#todolistfridays

Small Weekly Steps to Building a Big-Hearted Life

written by: don blackwell
illustrated and designed by: kc clark

Introduction

Several years ago, in the most unlikely of places and under the most unforeseeable of circumstances, a voice whispered seven words to my heart that marked the starting point of what has since become my life's mission.

The words? **"You were never meant to be here!"** The mission? To change my life and yours – or at least extend an invitation for you to take my hand and the first step on a journey that I believe has the power to change your life, and the lives of everyone in it.

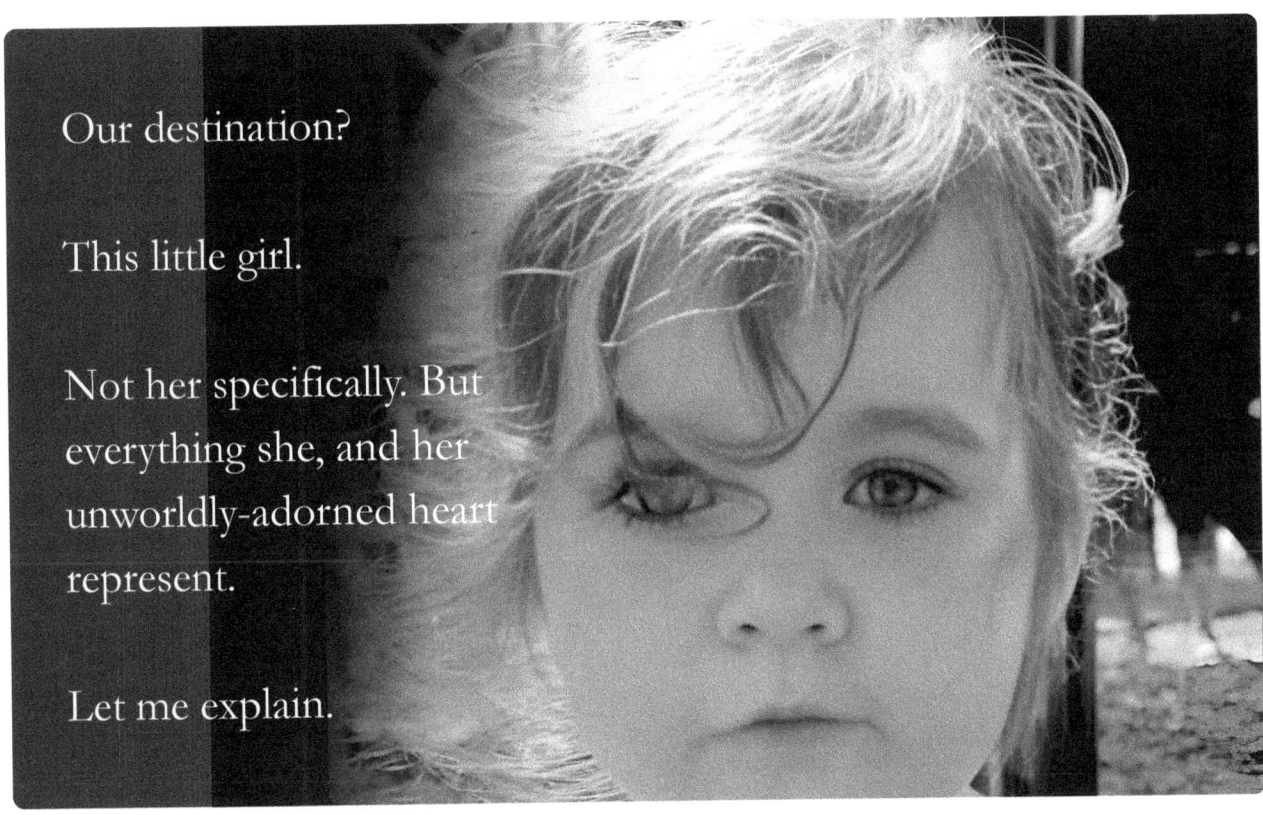

Our destination?

This little girl.

Not her specifically. But everything she, and her unworldly-adorned heart represent.

Let me explain.

You can search these eyes from now to eternity and you won't find a trace of self-loathing, hatred, anger, judgment, bigotry, jealousy, intolerance, perfectionism, harshness, criticism, rejection, exclusion, greed, pride, resentment, bitterness, prejudice, fear, unforgiveness, guilt, or shame.

What you will find instead are kindness, curiosity, warmth, gentleness, vulnerability, softness, authenticity, inclusiveness, spontaneity, awe, wonder, playfulness, self-acceptance, forgiveness, endless second chance coupons, a sense of adventure, and grace – limitless grace.

I know, because I've had the privilege of doing it.

Here's the thing: Once upon a time, not so long ago, these were your eyes too – and mine. We also shared her heart.

But something happened on the way to adulthood. Lots of things actually. Harsh things. Hurtful things. Hard things. Things that convinced us there was simply no place in an adult world for the soft pieces of us.

Instead, we came to believe that if we were going to survive, let alone thrive as adults we would need hard edges, leather tough skin, and titanium shells around our hearts.

And so, we hurriedly boxed up the few pieces of our childhood hearts that remained, like the remnants of a gourmet meal, placed them in the deep freeze, put on the bravest face we could find, and set out to conquer the world.

Eventually, in our busyness and obsessive desire to succeed, we forgot those pieces were even there and, with each passing year, we cared a little less.

As it turns out, we (and the world) were dead wrong.

The world doesn't need us to be less childlike, it needs us to be more childlike. It doesn't need harder hearts. It needs softer ones.

The good news is, those pieces of us are right where we left them – maybe encrusted in a little freezer burn, but none the worse for wear, and eager to be set free.

The challenge we face is to find our way back to them.

And that's the journey I hope to inspire you to take – **one Friday baby step at a time –** by sharing with you just some of what's waiting in store when you find your way home to the "you" that came into this world.

The "you" you were always meant to be.

A Note From the Author On How To Get The Most Out Of This Book

For the better part of the past two years, I have rather religiously posted on LinkedIn on Mondays and Fridays, under the monikers **#MondayMusings** and **#ToDoListFridays** in the hope that both would inspire readers to become a little more introspective and intentional in their pursuit of a more whole- and open-hearted life.

One day, a dear friend suggested I combine 52 of the latter posts in a single manuscript with an accompanying set of prompts designed to provide a broader community of readers young and old with yet another means of finding their way back to the uniquely beautiful hearts that accompanied all of us into this world.

As with its predecessor—The Playbook of Your Childhood Heart—there is no "right" way to enjoy this work. But I structured it the way I did hoping that, each Friday morning, readers would spend a few minutes reading the one item **#todolist** and then spend the week that follows reflecting and responding to the challenge it presents.

To help facilitate and encourage that approach, I have included a few suggested "Reflect & Respond" prompts **not with the idea that you will be overwhelmed by the thought of having to do all of them**, but in the hope that at least one will resonate with your heart and provide an impetus for journaling and growth.

That said, you are by no means "limited" to just those prompts. Your heart may have another idea in mind entirely, and if it does, you should follow its lead—ALWAYS. Rest assured, dozens of prompts already found their way onto the cutting room floor in the construction of this work!

Wishing you a patient, thoughtful, playful, and whimsical journey.

With Warmth and Gratitude,

#todolistfridays

Small Weekly Steps to Building a Big-Hearted Life

For permissions or inquiries, please contact:
Donald Blackwell
don@retuneyourheart.com
retuneyourheart.com

#todolistfridays Small Weekly Steps to Building a Big-Hearted Life
ISBN: 979-8-218-89649-2

First Edition: December 2025

Disclaimer:
This workbook is intended solely for educational and reflective purposes. It is not a substitute for professional advice or counseling. The publisher and authors disclaim any liability arising directly or indirectly from the use of this workbook.

Written by: Donald Blackwell
Designed and Illustrated by: KC Clark

#todolistfridays

Week One:
Skip the Fit

Macie loves to build blocks. The thing is she doesn't quite understand the concept or importance of a strong foundation. Consequently, more often than not, her meticulously built towers suddenly and quite dramatically come crashing down, leaving dozens of blocks strewn across the playroom floor.

When they do, I expect Macie to pitch a fit, especially given the time and patience she devotes to building her towers, and how obviously and rightfully pleased with (and proud of) herself she is with each block she manages to add without them collapsing—against all engineering odds (and several laws of physics).

In fact, through the years, I've seen plenty of adults (friends, lawyers, judges, teachers, parents, bosses, youth league coaches, spouses, etc.) pitch fits—even full on tantrums—over what, relatively speaking, were far less "traumatic" events. If I'm to be honest, I've even pitched a few (thousand) of them myself along the way.

What I haven't seen, however, is a single one of those fits—or the frustration, anger, alienation, expressions of disappointment, guilt, and shame that invariably accompany them—make a positive, life- or self-affirming difference in the pitcher or the pitchee. But I have seen and felt the hurt—and struggled to pick up the pieces (my own and others').

Macie seems to intuitively understand the futility of fits, because even when towers collapse around her, she doesn't lash out, throw things, scream, slam doors, or look for others to blame. She responds instead with hope and anticipation for what is to come, and 3 simple words: "**build it again**." And because she does, she creates "space" for new towers to be borne.

Imagine that. Now consider this. Once upon a time, your heart responded to adversity the same way. And, trust me, it longs to again.

An Invitation to

Reflect & Respond

Reflect on a time: (1) where you felt your emotions rising, and you paused instead of reacting; or (2) when something you built or worked for suddenly collapsed. Describe the emotions and what it revealed about your heart. Where in your life could you choose grace or a "build it again" spirit over frustration?

_____

_____

_____

_____

_____

_____

_____

_____

_____

_____

_____

_____

_____

_____

_____

_____

_____

_____

_____

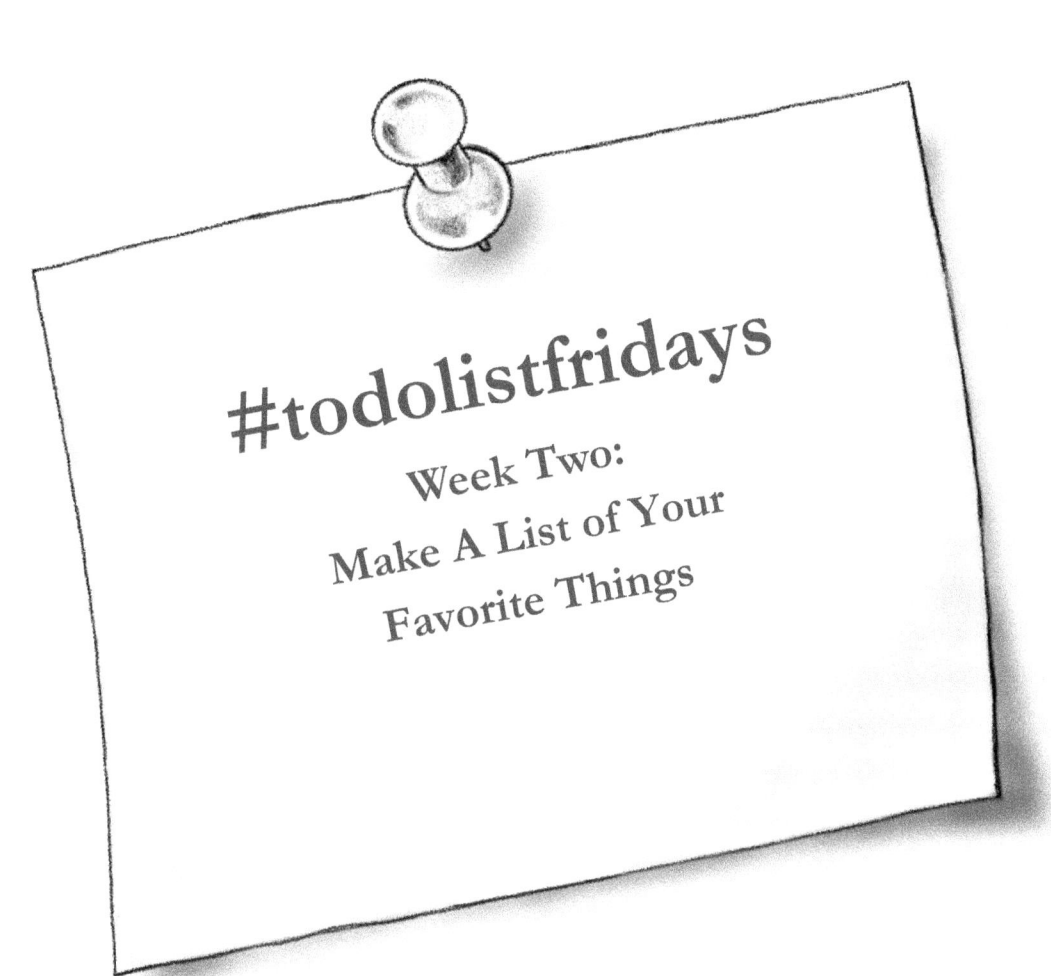

#todolistfridays

Week Two:
Make A List of Your
Favorite Things

"When the dog bites, when the bee stings, when I'm feeling sad, I simply remember my favorite things, and then I don't feel so bad." Sound of Music (1965)

I don't know about you, but the last things I tend to think about when I'm in a rut or feeling blue are "raindrops on roses," "whiskers on kittens," "bright copper kettles," "warm woolen mittens," "brown paper packages tied up with strings," or "wild geese that fly with the moon on their wings."

No, like most, when I'm stuck and feel the darkness setting in, my mind goes to "adult" things. I question my worthiness. I become fearful. I start to wonder what's wrong with me, what's missing, what I need to do more or less of, how I can feel so alone in a crowded space, where I misplaced me, my ability to laugh – my joy – what it will take to feel fully alive again.

But a few weeks back, as I watched Macie light up like a Christmas tree at the mere utterance of the question, "Do you want to go in the POOL?" and bolt for the door like the house was on FIRE, it occurred to me that, all those years ago, Julie Andrews may have been onto something, an elixir of sorts, a well-spring of nourishment to replenish depleted hearts – Favorite Things!

It also occurred to me that most of those "things" would be ones that remind us of childhood – of a time when we felt free to express ourselves, be ourselves, emote, engage, enjoy, explore, and experience the world and each other – fearlessly, unapologetically and honestly – when we found true joy in moments and people, rather than things.

I suspect everyone's Favorite Things are different, but each shares one important trait. In their presence, it is impossible to restrain our heart from brightening, from smiling; and therein lies their magic – the ability, if only for a moment, to introduce light, joy, safe harbor, and peace in the midst of a storm.

"What a remarkable gift that is," I thought to myself. And then I realized it was one that, with a little thought, I could (and probably should) give to myself. So, as soon as my play date with Macie was over, I sat down, pen in hand, and began scribbling away with heart smiles as my guide.

I encourage you to give it a try - and the next time you find yourself looking for something to do or are about to board the train to Bitterville, pull out your list, close your eyes, pick an item at random and remember what that feels, smells, tastes, sounds, or looks like! I dare you to keep from smiling.

P.S. In case you're curious, here's my list!

Any seat in Fenway Park.
Leaving the first set of footprints on a dew-covered fairway.
Blueberries.
A real hug.
Being the reason for someone else's smile.
The breadsticks at the Red Diamond Inn.
A wagging tail.
Any song by David Gates and Bread.
The Giving Tree.
"The Wright House" at Ocean Isle Beach.
Firsts.
Apple pie (no mode).
Og Mandino's writings.
A heart talk.
Hitting the sweet spot.
A comeback story.
Marvin Gaye's rendition of the Star-Spangled Banner at the NBA All-Star Game.
The smell of freshly mown grass.
An intimate kiss.
Mini-golf.

Climbing a dirt pile.
Watching children at play.
The North Grounds Softball Field at UVA Law School.
The Grotto at Notre Dame on a snowy night.
Dusk on the Spring Hill College golf course.
Long walks.
A freshly made waffle bowl.
Simon and Garfunkel.
An original 7-11 Icee (Cola).
Flipping baseball cards.
Red licorice.
Drying tears.
The Little Engine That Could.
Watching someone realize a lifelong dream.
A perfect strike.
Writing words that matter.

An Invitation to
Reflect & Respond

Make a list of the people, places, songs, food, and memories that make your heart smile.
What items on the list surprise you, shift your mood, lighten you—inspire hopefulness?
What will you add to the list in the coming week?

_____

_____

_____

_____

_____

_____

_____

_____

_____

_____

_____

_____

_____

_____

_____

_____

_____

_____

_____

_____

#todolistfridays

Week Three:
Practice Loveness

Chances are, at some point, we or someone we love will walk through a season of brokenness.

Some who are reading this are in different stages of one of those seasons right now.

The fact is, despite our best efforts and sacrifices –

"Sometimes things break. Sometimes we break them.

But it's not the breaking that matters - the how or why.

What matters is how we choose to respond to the brokenness.

Does it kill us?

Does it throw us into a downward spiral of blame, bitterness, regret, and punishment?

OR

Does it help us remember (or teach us) how to love deeper?

Does it push us towards compassion and over the hurdle of 'rightness' and 'wrongness' into LOVENESS? Yes. LOVENESS.

Go now ... Teach that. Show that. Live that.

It's called LOVENESS.

Go. NOW."

An excerpt from "Broken Things" by Kathleen Fleming

An Invitation to
Reflect & Respond

"Loveness" is about showing up with tenderness, generosity, and open-heartedness—especially when it's hardest. Recall a time when you practiced "loveness." How did it feel to lead with love? Where might love be asking for a seat at the table in your life right now?

_____

_____

_____

_____

_____

_____

_____

_____

_____

_____

_____

_____

_____

_____

_____

_____

_____

_____

_____

_____

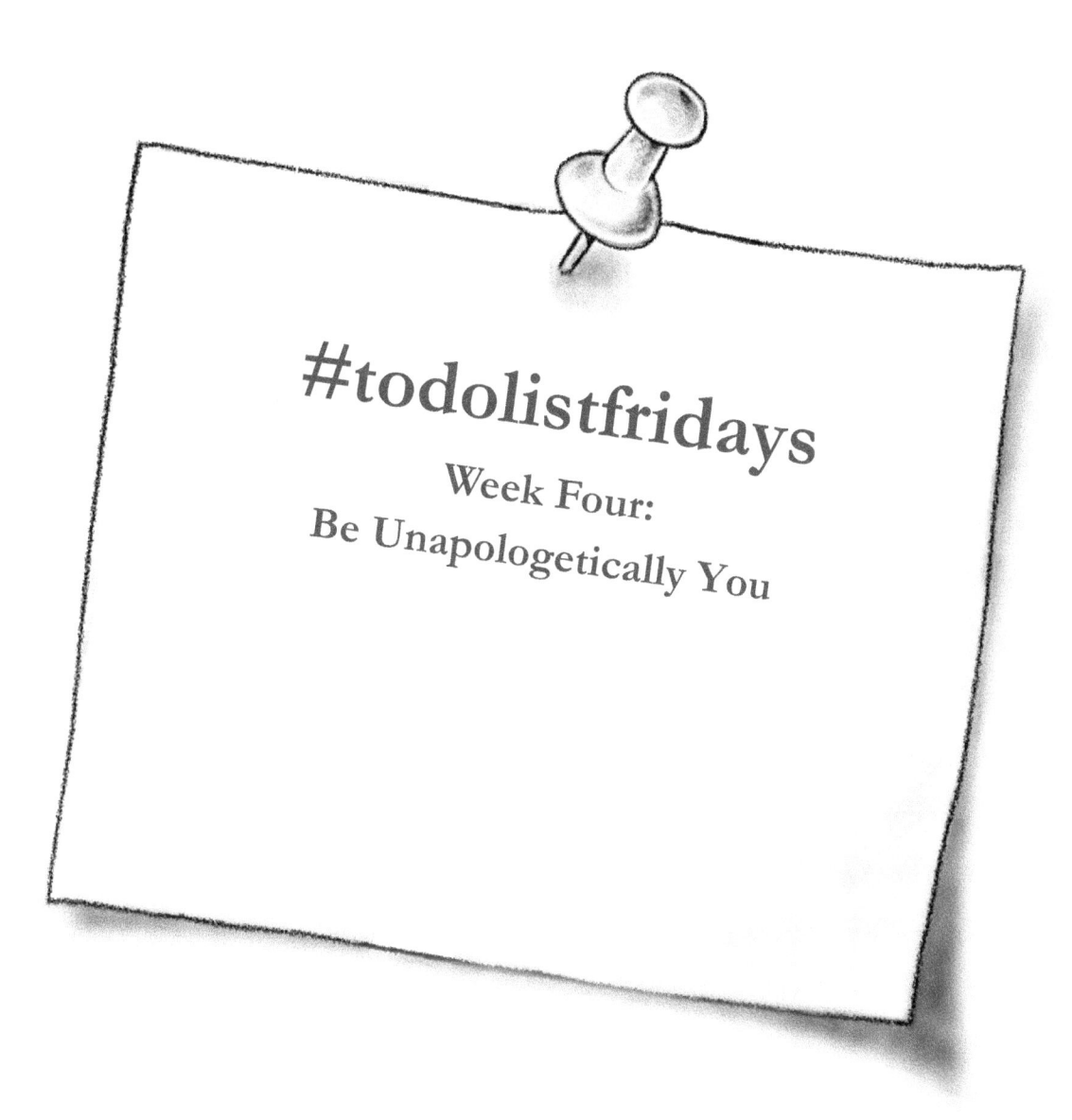

#todolistfridays

Week Four:
Be Unapologetically You

"This is who I am inside. This is who I am, I'm not gonna hide. Because the greatest risk we'll ever take is by far to stand in the light and be seen as we are." "Stand in the Light" (Jordan Smith)

When was the last time you "busted out" the adult equivalent of your favorite cow print skirt, threw on a semi-ragged, rainbow print T-shirt and a pair of purple crocs (with teal socks!), headed up to the neighborhood playground, played your butt off with a group of just-met friends, got drenched in sweat, grabbed a book out of the "sharing" box, and just plopped down in the middle of the sidewalk with your bestie to spend a minute letting your imagination run wild - all without giving a moment's thought to what others might think about any of it or you?

Macie did it two weeks ago - truth is, with a few variations on the theme, it's pretty much how she lives EVERY DAY - and here's what struck me. She was perfectly comfortable - indeed JOYFUL - in her own skin the entire time! As importantly, not a single one of the other kids at the park gave any of it - her fashion choices, the Florida humidity-induced frizzyness of her hair, her sweatiness, her impromptu decision to take a break from play and read a book, or the fact that she chose to read it in the middle of the sidewalk - a second thought. And they most certainly didn't stare or glare at her disapprovingly, make fun of her, call her unkind names, or, worse yet, ostracize her for it.

"How is that possible?" I wondered. And then it occurred to me. Their unbridled affection for Macie - and hers for herself - aren't contingent on any of those really-could-care-less things. Even the most new found of friends love Macie simply because she IS Macie. And Macie loves herself for the same reason. Here's a little secret: Once upon a time, you loved "you" and others with the same beautiful sense of reckless abandon and indifference to the trappings of worldliness. Imagine that.

Now imagine living and loving that way again, because you can. And if my recent visit to the park is any indication, it's a lifestyle well worth rediscovering!

An Invitation to
Reflect & Respond

Recall the last time you felt completely at ease just being yourself. What were you doing, and how did it feel? What aspects of "you" do you tend to hide or tone down for fear of being judged or rejected? What would it take to start letting those parts of you shine through again—or for the first time? What does "standing in the light and being seen as you are" mean to you? What's one concrete way you can "step into the light" in the coming week?

_____

_____

_____

_____

_____

_____

_____

_____

_____

_____

_____

_____

_____

_____

_____

_____

_____

_____

#todolistfridays

Week Five:
Reclaim Your Acoustic Self

"To be yourself in a world that is constantly trying to make you something else is the greatest accomplishment." Ralph Waldo Emerson

In her iconic 1972 song, Circle Game, the legendary Joni Mitchell lamented the fact that, once we're captive on "the Carousel of Time," we can't return to the uniquely beautiful, unworldly adorned hearts of our childhood - hearts that were filled with wonder at the simple sight of a dragonfly inside a jar, that were "fearful when the sky was full of thunder," and "tearful at the falling of a star."

Instead, to hear Mitchell tell it, we're relegated to simply looking longingly "behind from where we came" and continuing "round and round and round in the circle game."

For the longest time, I too subscribed to the belief that, once lost, the traits that characterized our unencumbered childhood hearts could never be recaptured and restored, that our progression from childhood to adulthood was linear and one directional.

But several years ago—in the most unlikely of places and under the most unforeseeable of circumstances—I had an epiphany.

I realized that, thankfully, Joni and I were wrong!

We not only can return to our Acoustic Self, we must. It's the only chance we have of experiencing the fullness of life we were meant to enjoy.

Let's do this—together!

An Invitation to

Reflect & Respond

When was the last time you felt like your true, "acoustic" self—free of performance, polish, or pressure? In what ways has the world tried to shape or silence your authentic voice? What keeps you from living fully as yourself? What's one small, intentional act you could incorporate each day this week that honors the traits of your unfiltered, childhood self?

_____

_____

_____

_____

_____

_____

_____

_____

_____

_____

_____

_____

_____

_____

_____

_____

_____

_____

_____

#todolistfridays

Week Six:

Become a Stripper

"Change" has lots of negative connotations, particularly when it comes to our person-hood. No matter how well-intentioned it may be in the offering, the phrase "I think you need to change" is typically heard as conveying one of the following messages: "You're just not good enough the way you are, and unless and until you become the person I think you should be, I can't/won't continue to support or love you;" "There's a piece missing in 'you' that needs to be filled in order for me to be your friend and I suggest you get busy figuring out what it is, where to find it, and how to put it in place before it's too late;" or, worse yet, "I can't quite put my finger on it, but you're deficient or 'defective' in some way and we need to figure out a way to 'correct' that."

Don't get me wrong, there likely are times when those messages are the ones the sender actually intends to convey, and when that's the case, I encourage you to run, not walk, away from that person as quickly as possible! But I believe real change is less about becoming a "new" or "different" person and more about the process of returning to a former, truer version of us. What I like to call our Acoustic Self. Simply put, rather than the "putting on" of something new, change actually is the stripping away of layers of "contaminants" that have been thrust upon us or that we have acquired and/or taken on over the years that have obscured from view or altered the person we were intended and came into this world to be.

Viewed in this light, the call to change is a far more adventurous and far less threatening/intimidating process than the one we typically associate with the word and the accompanying journey. This is not to say that it is any less challenging! To the contrary, anyone who has ever gotten lost on a hike or in a foreign land will readily attest to the difficulties and anxiety associated with finding their way back home. Still, knowing that it's "home" (and everything that goes with it) that you're striving to return to and that the little girl or boy in you is waiting with open arms (and a longing to be set free) makes the process considerably more tolerable than continuing on a path into the unknown.

Chances are your 4-year-old self didn't aspire to be "a stripper," let alone imagine that he or she would one day have to "strip" to find the joy that flowed so freely and spontaneously from their unworldly-adorned heart. Then again, they never could have imagined what would become of that heart once the world took hold of it and obscured that joy – and so many of its other uniquely beautiful characteristics - from view. So, stripping it is!

28

An Invitation to
Reflect & Respond

What feelings or memories does the word "change" bring up for you? How might reframing it as "stripping away" instead of "adding on" shift your perspective? What emotional or identity "layers" have you taken on over the years that no longer serve you and are ready to be stripped away? In what ways have you drifted away from your most authentic self because of worldly expectations? What is one step you can take this week to reclaim you?

_____

_____

_____

_____

_____

_____

_____

_____

_____

_____

_____

_____

_____

_____

_____

_____

_____

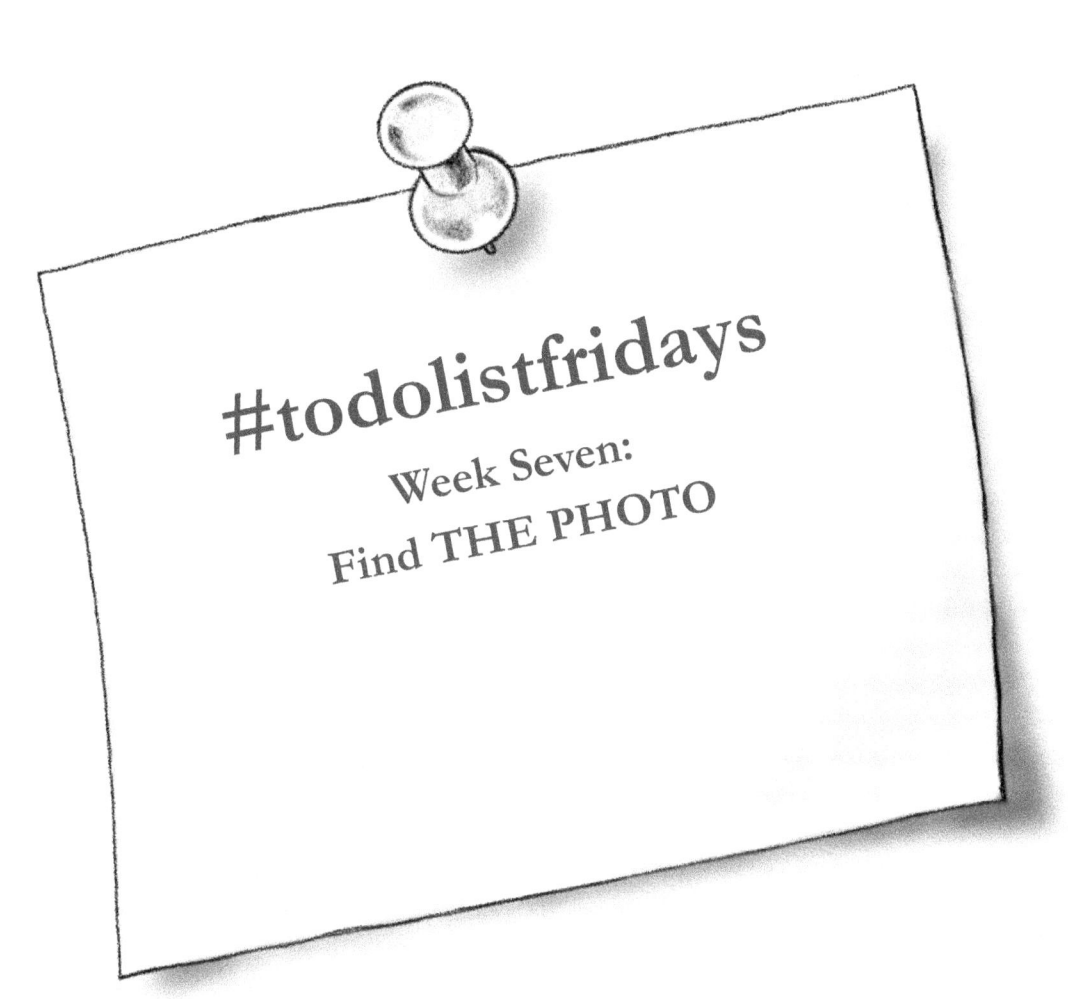

#todolistfridays
Week Seven:
Find THE PHOTO

All of us have one – a favorite photograph.

An image of us or of a loved one (or both) that, no matter how often we look at it, brings a smile to our face or prompts tears of joy to well up in our eyes.

A moment – frozen in time – when life seemed to make perfect sense, when the pieces of the puzzle more neatly fit together, when our minds and our lives were less cluttered, less busy, when we felt free and unashamed to be silly, to just be our unadorned, authentic selves – to speak and share our truth without hesitation.

Maybe yours depicts a moment of PEACE, unfiltered JOY, CONNECTION, ACCOMPLISHMENT, ANTICIPATION, or PLAYFULNESS.

Whatever the moment, its power is real. In seemingly impenetrable darkness it is a sliver of light. In the quicksand of despair it is a lifeline of hope. In the stormy seas of self-doubt it is a lighthouse of love. In the midst of chaos it is comfort.

Most importantly, contrary to what our Inner Critic would have us believe and however dire they may appear, it serves as irrefutable evidence that our present circumstances are not the way our life has always been, nor are they how it is likely to be going forward.

A few years ago, I received a note from a young woman I'd been corresponding with for several months. She'd been battling her demons for a long time, and it was a particularly dark and difficult day. "I'm tired of the fight," she said, "really tired – of everything. I want to give up."

Had there not been 2,000 miles between us, I would've dropped everything and rushed to her side to hold her heart in my arms and reaffirm its worthiness. Instead, I texted her back: "Do you have a favorite photograph?" I asked, "an image of you taken at a simpler time, when you were happy, healthy and carefree that you're especially fond of?" "Yes," she replied without hesitation.

"Then please put down the phone," I said. "Find it and place it somewhere where you'll be sure to see it several times a day." "Why?" she asked. "Because the 'you' in that photo hasn't gone anywhere! She's just waiting for you to find your way back to her and set her free." "It's just so hard," she replied. "I know," I said. "It's likely the hardest thing you'll ever do. But that girl in the photo is counting on you. Make her your inspiration— and begin a real life game of hide and seek!"

Ready or not . . .

An Invitation to
Reflect & Respond

What photo comes to mind when you read this? Where were you? Who were you with? What emotions does the photo capture? When was the last time you truly felt that way? How does the "you" in that photo differ from the "you" today? Where can you place the photo so it becomes a daily reminder of who you are and the joy you're capable of? Allow its presence to shift your energy, choices, and conversations this week.

_____

_____

_____

_____

_____

_____

_____

_____

_____

_____

_____

_____

_____

_____

_____

_____

_____

_____

_____

#todolistfridays

Week Eight:
Acknowledge Your
Limitations

Trust me, we all have them.

It's easy to deceive ourselves into believing that ours are the only hands on the rudder of our life's ship, especially when the seas are smooth, and the wind is at our back. I've naively done it myself - about a million times.

But, thankfully, they're not, at least I don't believe they are, because there are some storms that even the most skilled of sailors can't safely navigate without help.

Maybe today you find yourself in one of those storms.

Maybe it's raging and you feel as if the boat you're in is taking on water faster than you can bail it out.

Maybe part of you even feels like there's no way out – that "drowning" in it all is inevitable. It's not! I promise.

But if that's where you are, it's likely going to take more than just you to find a safe harbor – a moment's respite.

It starts with setting aside our pride, acknowledging our limitations, and reaching out for help. If you're a person of faith, it includes surrendering to a love beyond our understanding.

If you're not, it's reaching out to a family member, spouse, friend, help line, or colleague at work, and continuing to reach out until a life-preserver is cast – and then humbly and gratefully embracing it.

In the meantime, know that you are loved, that there's a random guy in Miami who sees and believes in you, and that you are not alone.

An Invitation to
Reflect & Respond

What "storm" are you currently facing that feels overwhelming? What emotions surface when you think about it? In what areas of your life do you tend to hold tightly to the rudder? How has the need to control helped or hurt you? What "life preservers" (habits, people, practices, or moments of grace) have saved you in past storms and which ones could you reach out to this week? What's stopping you, and how could you push through that resistance?

_____

_____

_____

_____

_____

_____

_____

_____

_____

_____

_____

_____

_____

_____

_____

_____

_____

_____

#todolistfridays

Week Nine:

Be Love

We've lost our way. We've lost sight of what we're doing on this magnificent planet - or at least what we're supposed to be doing - LOVING. It's both that simple and that complicated.

I'm not talking about loving when it's easy, although that's just as beautiful and as necessary. I'm talking about loving when it's hard - loving harder, loving as completely and sacrificially as the circumstances require.

We weren't created to be sowers of hate, conflict, and discontent. We are called to be purveyors of hope and light. Stepping off my tiny virtual soapbox now - and going back to loving ... like a 4-year-old.

Let Me Be Love (A Prayer) (Adapted from Rachel Macy Stafford's, "Only Love Today")

Dear God,

Let me be love. Not the shiny, perfectly worded, flashy, flowery love that comes when it's convenient and goes when it's not.

No, let me be the messy, genuine, put in the effort, feel it in your bones, "Come As You Are" kind of love.

Let me be the Show Up kind of love that is found where it is least expected and when it is most needed.

Let me be the Mountain Moving kind of love that offers and inspires hope and makes growth possible.

Let me be the Unconditional, Limitless kind of love that rises with the sun and stretches beyond human failings and shortcomings.

Let me be the Lighthouse kind of love, a beacon of light in the swirling storms of life that leads to a safe and peaceful harbor.

Let me be the All-In kind of love that risks it all, holds nothing back, and encourages honesty and transparency.

Let me be the Wholly-Accepting, Open-Hearted kind of love that makes for a soft place to lay one's head at night for both the giver and the receiver.

Let me be that love. Amen.

An Invitation to
Reflect & Respond

Who in your life might benefit from you being a "lighthouse of love" right now? What holds you back from offering love whole and open heartedly? How can you gently let go of those limitations and love more freely this week? Who brings out the "all-in, no-holds-barred" love in you? What would it look like to let that love spill out into the rest of your life?

_____

_____

_____

_____

_____

_____

_____

_____

_____

_____

_____

_____

_____

_____

_____

_____

_____

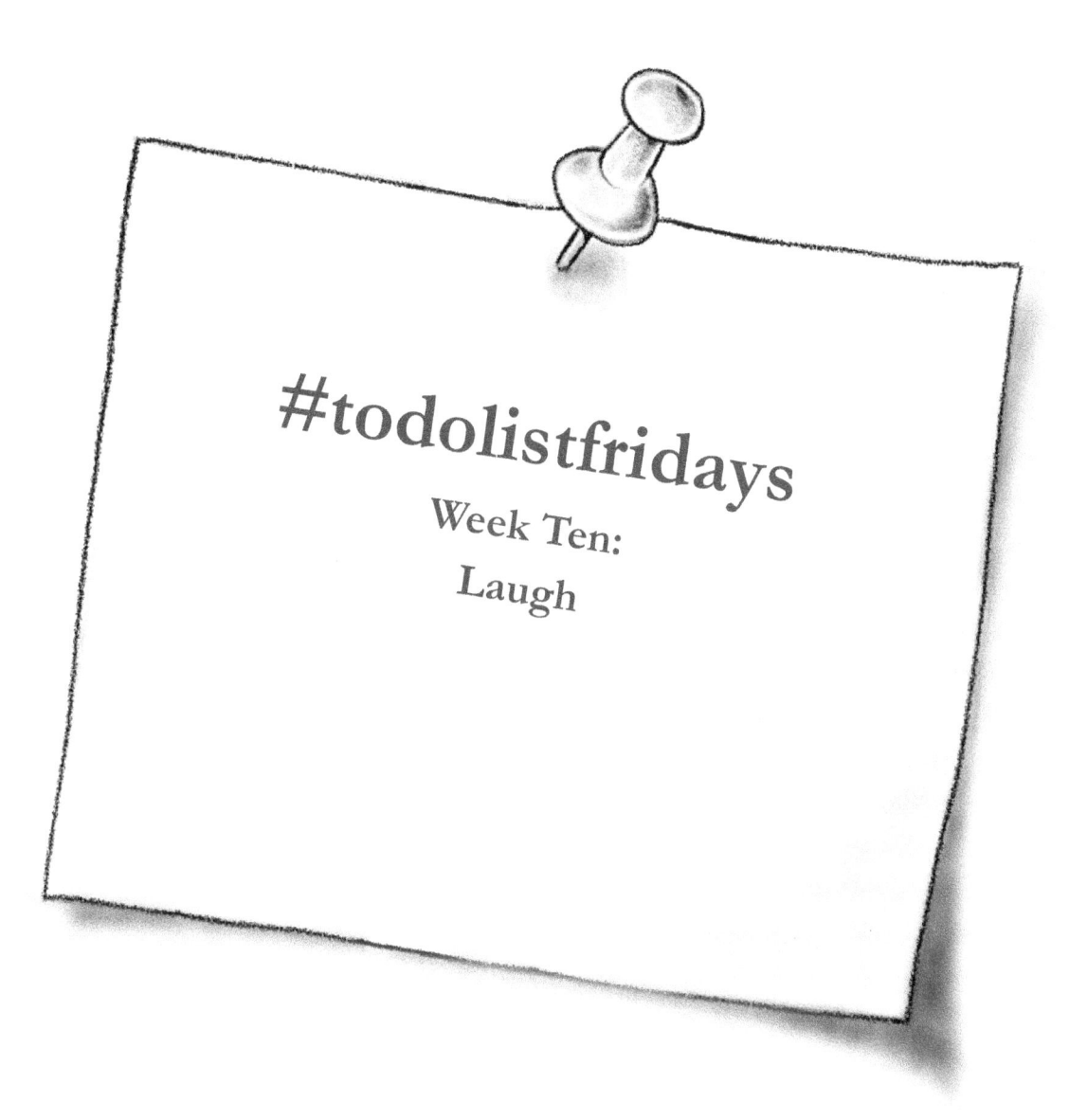

#todolistfridays

Week Ten:

Laugh

There's nothing like the sound of a child's laughter to remind us that, once upon a time, Life didn't feel as heavy, noisy, overwhelming, and complicated as it does for far too many of us these days.

And it wasn't.

Truth is, Life was never intended to be many of the things that, as adults, we insist on making it – or allowing it to be.

Recently, after a morning visit to the park, I decided that the letters of Macie's alphabet puzzle wanted to join in the fun and, one by one, go down a makeshift "slide" I created in the playroom.

Being the ever-the-contrarian, 3-year-old Macie is, A and B never quite made it past "Ready, Set . . ." before they were pushed back up the sofa bumper turned slide into my face!

But the laughter that ensued was EVERYTHING – spontaneous, playful, irreverent, joyful, contagious, and liberating – and it didn't end until all 26 letters had their turn!

Take a moment to find laughter like that in your own life this week, and let it take up residence in your soul, so that your heart can be reminded what it feels like.

Who knows maybe a reminder is all the permission it needs to break out in laughter itself at the simplest and silliest of invitations to joyfulness that are all around us.

An Invitation to
Reflect & Respond

When was the last time you laughed until tears filled your eyes? What sparked it? Who were you with? Who are the people who consistently bring laughter into your life? Are you making time for them? If not, why not? How does laughter change your thoughts, posture, and energy? What steps can you take this week to make more space for that version of you more often?

_____

_____

_____

_____

_____

_____

_____

_____

_____

_____

_____

_____

_____

_____

_____

_____

_____

_____

_____

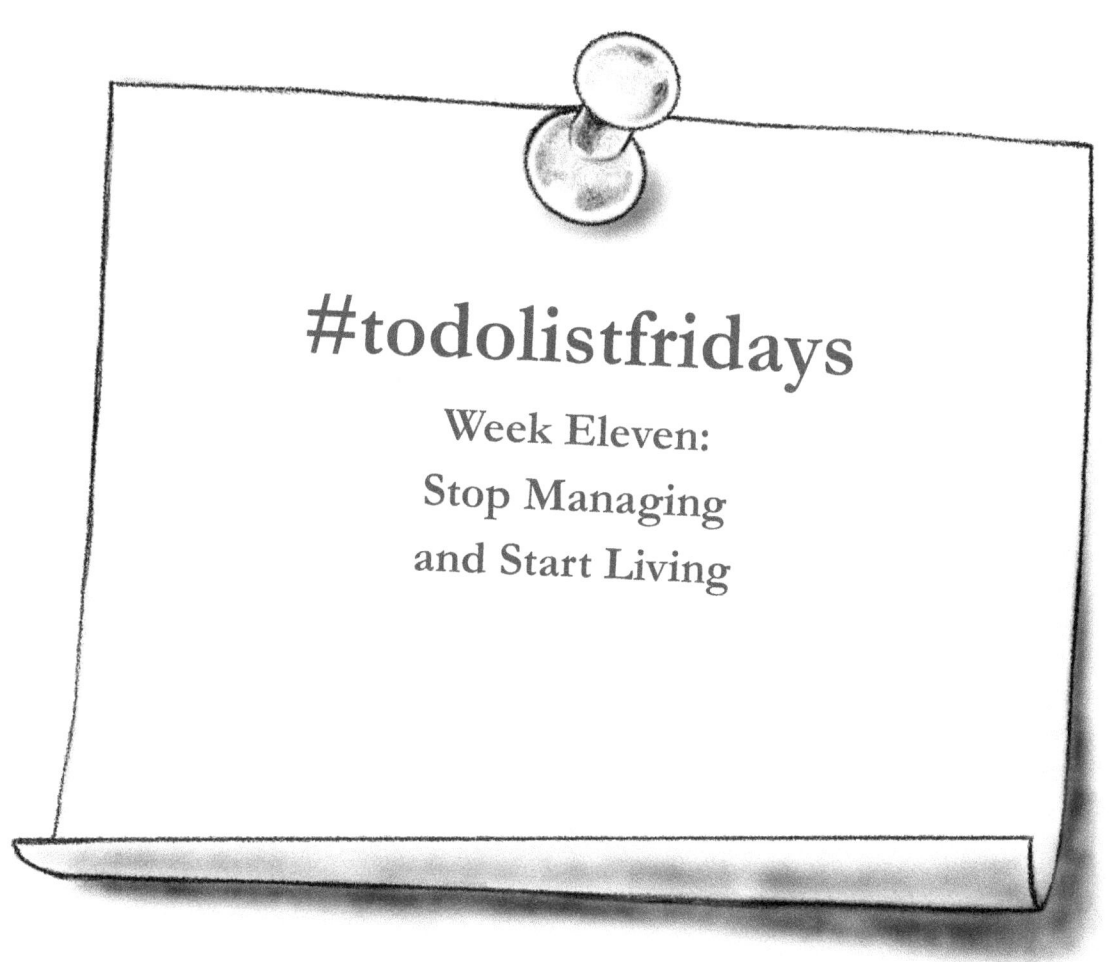

#todolistfridays

Week Eleven:
Stop Managing
and Start Living

Early one Sunday morning, we made the 40-minute drive from Titusville to New Smyrna Beach as part of a weeks-in-the-making PLAN to take Macie to "The Beach" for the very first time. As "fate" would have it, however, though the weather forecast (monitored carefully for days and checked only minutes before we walked out the door) called for "morning sunshine followed by afternoon showers," it rained the entire time we were there – 9:00 am to 10:30 am.

The adults (save for yours truly!) were mostly and quite understandably "miserable" given that the weather had "ruined OUR PLAN." The thing is, Macie had the time of her life! She laughed, played, and splashed in the "little waves," celebrated the raindrops like they were gumdrops, sang "Row, Row, Row Your Boat" 100 times (all while watching her tiny plastic sailboat repeatedly "take on water" and sink!), and ran up and down the wet sand like she was auditioning for "Chariots of Fire."

In an attempt to "salvage" the day, the adults then turned the lunch we had PLANNED at a local dockside restaurant into brunch, where Macie promptly befriended: a waitress who, attentively recognizing her love of fruit, "opened" a veritable blueberry and strawberry all-you-eat buffet; a little girl at the table next door whose bright pink, Frozen-themed sandals identified her as a kindred spirit; and "Fisherman Phil," who, as if on cue, caught a cute little catfish off the side of the dock – the first fish out-of-water Macie had ever seen.

As we headed for home, I couldn't help but reflect on how different Macie's perspective and experience of the day had been from the adults – and how many beautifully wrapped gifts would've been left unopened under the Christmas Tree of Life had mom, dad, Papa Don, and Nana known the actual weather forecast and never left their respective houses. It was then that I realized that it was the difference between our very adult desire/need to try to MANAGE life and Macie's zest for ACTUALLY LIVING IT!

You see, Macie had and has only one PLAN – and it NEVER changes. She LOVES life – ferociously and unconditionally – and she insists on siphoning every last drop of it out of EVERY day – rain or shine. No exceptions. She simply refuses to be denied or knocked off her stride by the vagaries of something as trivial and unavoidable as the weather. Make no mistake. Once upon a time, you and I lived and loved the same way – joyfully, spontaneously, playfully, and unapologetically.

It's just that somewhere along the way we lost sight of what that way of living looks and feels like. That day, I got a refresher course taught by a 2-year-old. And I'm here to tell you, it's pretty amazing!

An Invitation to
Reflect & Respond

Recall a time when things didn't go "according to plan." How did you respond? Looking back, did anything beautiful emerge from the disruption? In what areas of your life do you feel the strongest need to try and "manage" the outcome? What would letting go just a little look and feel like? Are there "rainy day" moments in your life right now that you've been seeing only as obstacles? Is it possible that something unexpected and beautiful might be hiding in them? If you rewrote your "plan" for this week using only Macie's philosophy, what would it say? How would that version of your week look and feel compared to your current one? What's one thing you can do to adopt that mindset today?

_____

_____

_____

_____

_____

_____

_____

_____

_____

_____

_____

_____

_____

_____

_____

_____

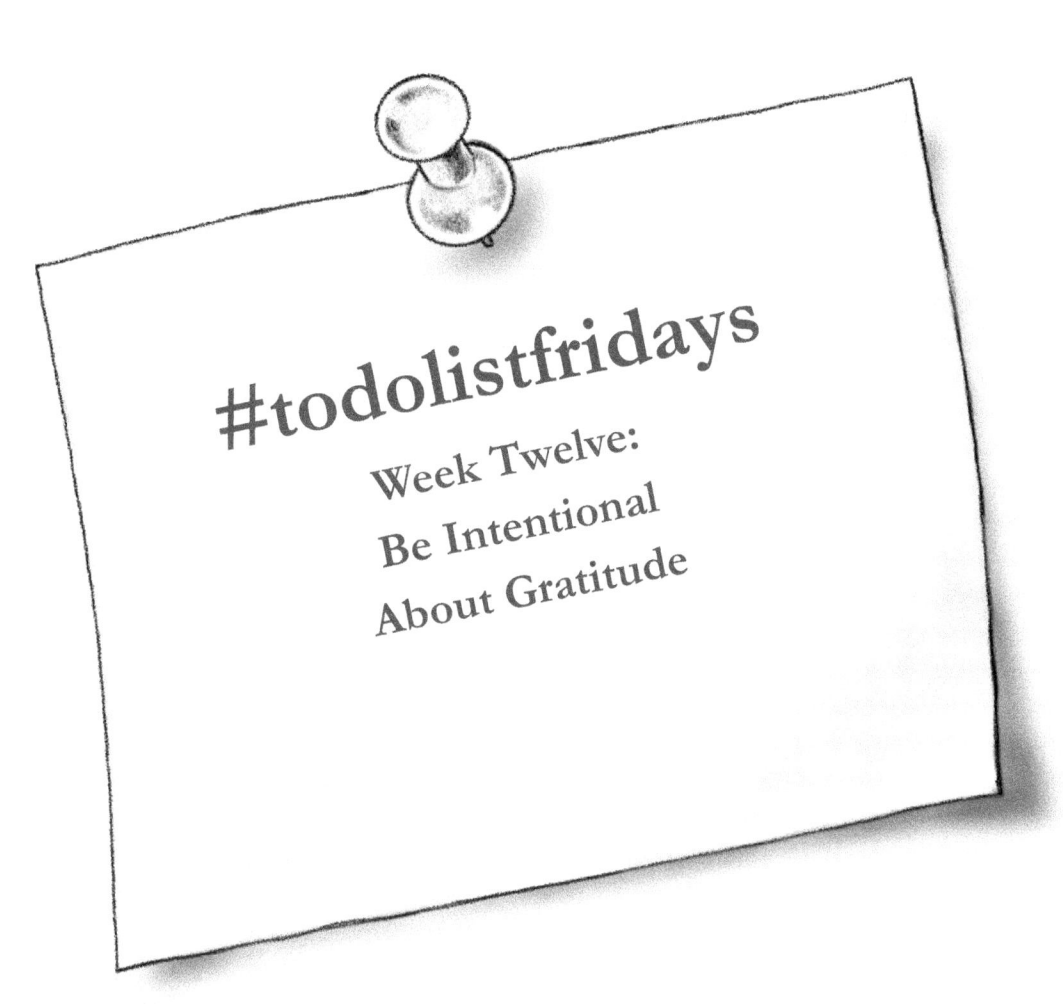

#todolistfridays

Week Twelve:
Be Intentional
About Gratitude

I don't know about you, but, for me, living in gratitude is not something that just happens.

Like most things that matter, it requires daily - sometimes hourly - intentionality.

Take today, for example. Before I could even formulate a thought around gratitude (*i.e.,* at 7:30 a.m.), I realized all the priceless gifts I'd already taken mostly for granted …

the first conscious breath of the day,
the miracle of Life itself,
a secure roof over my head,
a warm comfortable bed,
a restful night's sleep,
the realization that there are people in the world who love me,
a hot shower,
indoor plumbing,
clothes to wear,
a morning meal,
my health,
all 5 senses (still serviceably intact),
freedom – to travel, speak, practice my faith,
a job to go to,
a way to get there,
the right to vote,
grace and new mercies poured out,
a beautiful tapestry in the sky,
and all a new day carries with it (a second (or third!) chance, a fresh start, hope, the prospect of meeting a new friend or hearing from an old one, an opportunity to extend or receive forgiveness, etc.) …

to name just a few.

Truth is: We're quick to blow right past all that on our way to "too busy to notice" and quicker still to be critical – of ourselves and others.

Maybe this week, we can try a different approach: One that focuses first on the beauty and brilliance that is in us, in others, and in so much of what surrounds us – and pause long enough to be grateful.

An Invitation to
Reflect & Respond

What are three "ordinary" things in your life that are actually quite extraordinary when you sit with them? When was the last time you felt truly grateful for someone or something? Where have you been more critical than grateful lately—toward yourself, someone else, or a situation? What might compassion and gratitude look like in that place? What pulls my attention away from gratitude most often—busyness, worry, comparison, or habit? How can you create small spaces of stillness in your day to notice again?

_____

_____

_____

_____

_____

_____

_____

_____

_____

_____

_____

_____

_____

_____

_____

_____

_____

_____

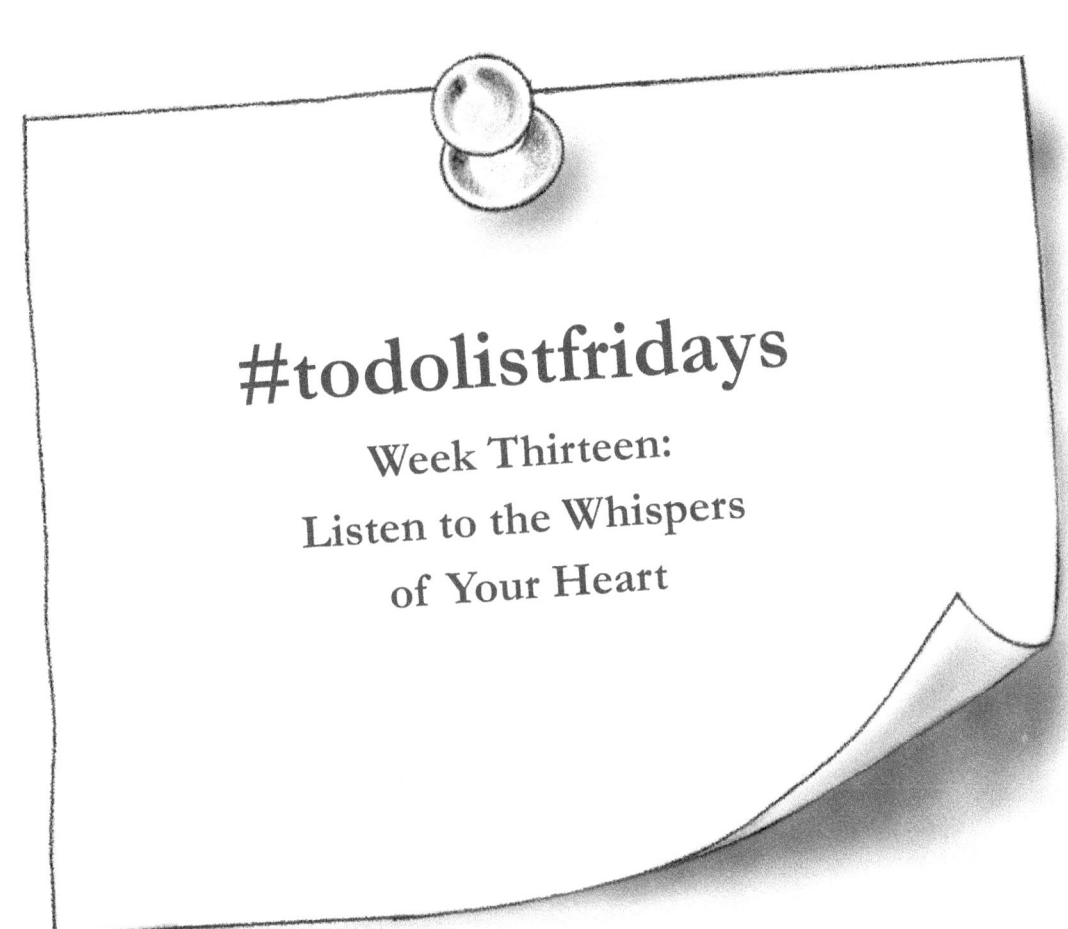

#todolistfridays

Week Thirteen:
Listen to the Whispers
of Your Heart

Several years ago, in a room filled with young and not-so-young men and women from all walks of life battling or in varying stages of recovery from addictions to every imaginable substance and behavior, I was handed a microphone, asked "if I had anything I wanted to say."

Truth be told, I was there to support a loved one, and, until that moment, was intent and perfectly content to remain invisible. I certainly hadn't planned on speaking. But, a split second later, I heard myself utter seven words that would forever change my life.

The thing is, at the time, I had absolutely no idea where those words came from or what I would say next. What was immediately clear to me, however, from the could've-heard-a-pin-drop silence that accompanied them was that there was a hand much bigger than mine at work in that space and my job was simply to surrender to it and serve as its mouthpiece.

But it took the birth of my now nearly 3-year-old granddaughter, Macie for me to connect the dots, and realize that those seven words—"you were never meant to be here"—were meant as much for me as the others who were gathered in that room.

What began as a faint, barely discernable whisper in my heart in the most unlikely of places and under the most unforeseeable of circumstances has since become three books, two workbooks, a website, and a message of hope and healing that are my purpose in life.

I'm eternally grateful I paid attention to it and, when you hear similar whispers in your own heart, I encourage you to do the same! Trust me, they're there.

An Invitation to
Reflect & Respond

Can you recall a time when something inside nudged you—gently, unexpectedly—to speak, act, or change direction? What happened? Did you follow it, or push it aside? What keeps you from trusting those gentle inner messages—fear, uncertainty, the noise of others' opinions? What would help you begin to distinguish, pay attention to, and risk acting on the true whispers of your heart? What practices, space, or habits help you get still enough to hear the whispers of your heart? What's one step you can take this week to allow more time and space to hear them? Is there something in your life that started small or quietly but has since grown into something bigger—something meaningful? How did it start, and what has it become?

_____

_____

_____

_____

_____

_____

_____

_____

_____

_____

_____

_____

_____

_____

_____

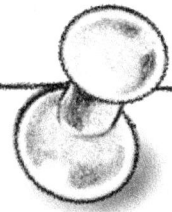

#todolistfridays

Week Fourteen:
Dispel the Notion that
There's a "Right" Way to do Life's
Hardest Things - Because There Isn't

The older I get, the clearer it becomes that there is no "right" way to navigate some of Life's biggest challenges:

- parenting a child,
- being a not-going-anywhere-no-matter-what kind of friend,
- walking alongside a loved one struggling with physical or mental illness (or struggling with either or both yourself),
- filling in the gaps/holes/chasms left behind by childhood wounds,
- getting up off the metaphorical canvas after a blow you never saw coming, grieving the loss of a piece of our heart

to name just a few.

At the end of the day, all any of us can do is the best we can do, given the tools, knowledge, and life experiences we've acquired along the way and, hopefully, the wisdom shared by those who have imperfectly walked similar paths before us, and learned from their missteps.

Realizing that has led me to two important takeaways.

First, we need to be more empathetic and forgiving to those who may not have gotten those things "as right" as we would've liked/hoped when we were on the receiving end of their striving.

Second, when we are/were the strivers, we need to cut ourselves a little slack and offer ourselves a lot more grace for the times we didn't (or don't) do some or all of those things as perfectly as we intended.

Because my experience has been that somewhere in the debris field created by our and others' imperfection is where real growth resides.

By the way, if it's any comfort, I've been at this Life thing a long time and I'm still learning to do both!

An Invitation to
Reflect & Respond

Think back to a time in your life when you were struggling despite doing the best you could and being criticized or overly critical of yourself. What would it have felt like to receive unconditional grace in that moment? From whom did you need it most? When have you chosen to extend grace to someone who hurt, disappointed, or failed you? What made it possible for you to do so? How did that act shape your relationship—or your own growth? Why are you so reluctant to extend that same grace to yourself? What's one simple act of grace you can offer yourself this week? What's one act of grace you can offer someone else? How can you make both habits rather than exceptions?

_____

_____

_____

_____

_____

_____

_____

_____

_____

_____

_____

_____

_____

_____

_____

_____

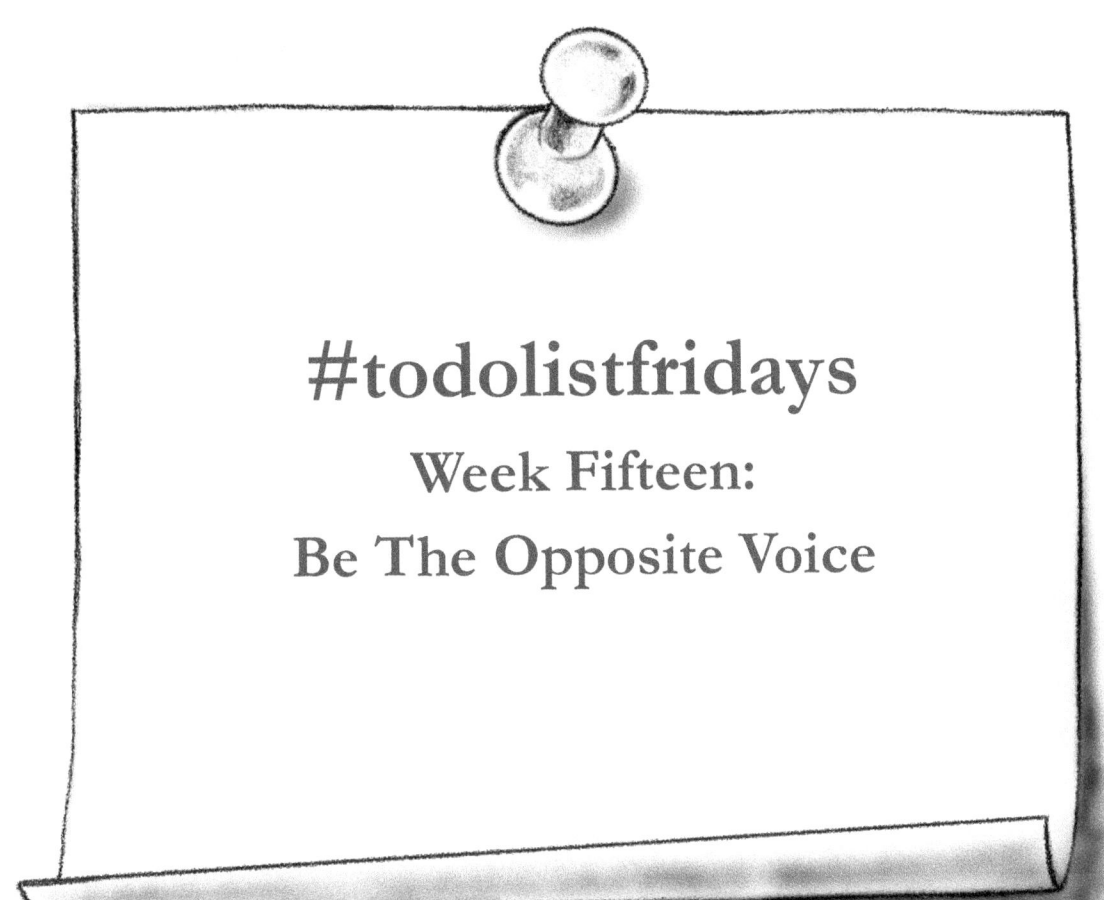

#todolistfridays
Week Fifteen:
Be The Opposite Voice

There is a voice inside all of us that is demeaning and hyper-critical.

It would have us believe many things about ourselves – that we are unloved, that we are not worthy of love, that the guilt and shame we all carry with us over past missteps are well-founded, that we are incapable of the task at hand, let alone of greatness.

It is a litany of lies and distortions, but, left unrebutted, it can have serious, even fatal consequences.

For that reason, it is imperative we have someone in our corner who is fully committed to instilling in us an Opposite Voice, one that acknowledges and validates our struggles, fears, self-doubt, sense of inadequacy and pain, while simultaneously encouraging and coaxing us to move forward.

At times, the Opposite Voice will need to be soft and reassuring – almost comforting. At other times, when our journey grows more difficult and the voice of self-doubt and unworthiness become persistent to the point of defiance, the Opposite Voice will need to become louder, more emphatic and unequivocal.

In all instances, however, the goal is simple, but critical.

Ultimately, the Opposite Voice has to drown out its hurtful and self-limiting counterpart just long enough for us to catch a glimpse of our true potential, and hopefully, create a desire to catch another glimpse, and another, and another.

We can help by being that voice for someone in need. And throw a hug in while you're at it - a REAL one!

An Invitation to
Reflect & Respond

What are some of the recurring messages your Inner Critic tells you and what seems to trigger them? Where do you think those messages originated? How often do you accept them without question? Think of one self-limiting belief you've carried for too long. What evidence in your life contradicts it? Can you name it for what it is—a distortion, not a truth? Can you recall a time in your life when you really could've benefited from an Opposite Voice? What did you wish it had said and who did you need to hear it from? What would it have meant to hear it? In what situations do you find it hardest to silence the critical voice? What would it take for your Opposite Voice to become louder, more insistent, and less willing to back down in those moments?

_____

_____

_____

_____

_____

_____

_____

_____

_____

_____

_____

_____

_____

_____

_____

#todolistfridays
Week Sixteen:
Be On the Lookout for the
Beautiful and When You Find It,
Which You Will Because It's
Everywhere, Acknowledge It

Several months ago, I was deeply touched by the sight a young mother and her son at a restaurant where I was having dinner.

It was beautiful beyond description.

"That young man will never go on a long walk questioning whether his mother loves him or why she didn't - or couldn't," I thought to myself.

"He will never know that pain, that sense of emptiness, the feelings of not enoughness, of unworthiness - or shed the tears borne of it."

I wondered if she realized the pricelessness of the gifts her heart, her smile, her touch, and her undivided attention were bestowing on her little man.

I hoped my buying them dinner (anonymously) helped her to see it, to know just how special she is, and that others notice.

An Invitation to
Reflect & Respond

What is one beautiful moment—no matter how small—you noticed today? Who or what was involved, and why did it move you? Reflecting on the story of the young mother and her son, was there ever a time you longed to be noticed, nurtured, or reassured like that? What would it have meant to have someone see and express your worth so clearly? Think of someone in your life who is quietly doing something you see as beautiful. Have you told them? How could you celebrate or acknowledge them this week—through words, gestures, or even anonymously? Do you believe others have noticed something beautiful in you that you don't always see in yourself? What steps can you take this week to be more attentive to the "beautiful" in and around you?

_____

_____

_____

_____

_____

_____

_____

_____

_____

_____

_____

_____

_____

_____

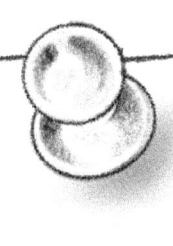

#todolistfridays

Week Seventeen:

Hide Less. Seek More.

When asked how he was able to create the iconic sculpture, David, Michelangelo replied, "I simply removed the pieces that weren't necessary."

I was never very good at Hide and Seek. Don't get me wrong, it wasn't the "hiding" piece I struggled with. To the contrary, I could contort my body (and, as the years went on, my heart) into nooks and crannies that would virtually guarantee I'd never be found. No, it was the "seeking" part – the pursuit - that made me grow to detest the game. It seemed that no matter how broadly or narrowly I drew the geographic boundaries for hiding I could never find anyone.

Maybe my friends were just that clever. Maybe 10 seconds is longer than it seems when it comes to disappearing from view. None of this bodes well for the journey I've embarked on - setting out in search of the better (acoustic) part of me. After all, if 10 seconds is a long time, imagine giving "me" – the Hider Extraordinaire – a 50-year head start.

But, I've decided I have to at least try to find "that guy" again, the one who dreamed big, knew no limits, felt intensely, crammed every day full, never felt the need to put on the mantle of having everything under control, was free to create, often lost himself in music and writing, and lived a simple, albeit somewhat predictable life.

I want to figure out what happened to him, where he's been hiding all these years, what forced him to feel like he needed to hide in the first place – and I want to set him free. I appreciate the risks. In fact, I've counseled others against looking, let alone going back, because too often it turns into a litany of "would'ves, could'ves and should'ves" – and the regrets that necessarily come with them. But the journey I'm envisioning will be different.

My hope is that this will be more David-like, akin to an "unveiling" of what I've only recently come to realize was an already existing "masterpiece" - a unique work of art that somewhere along the way got corrupted, neglected, and painted over such that much of its true beauty was lost or at least obscured from view.

Why? Because along the way, its owner decided "the picture" needed changing – that it wasn't quite good enough, desirable enough, loveable enough, or (you-fill-in-the-blank) enough. In my mind's eye, this will be a journey of rediscovering the good, accepting the not-so-good and offering myself a little grace), gaining understanding, and, hopefully, finding forgiveness. It's time that guy came out of hiding.

Maybe it's time all of us did. So, ready or not, here I come!

An Invitation to
Reflect & Respond

Think about when you started to hide. Was there a moment, a comment, a failure, or a loss that made "hiding" feel safer? What were you afraid might happen if you stayed visible? In what ways are you still hiding today emotionally, spiritually, creatively, etc.? What would it look like to take one small step out of that hiding place this week? Like Michelangelo's David, what "pieces" of you might not be necessary anymore—old stories, defenses, roles, or identities that obscure the masterpiece underneath that is you? What would it mean—for you, and for the people who love you—if you stopped hiding and started living more fully as your truest self? What might the unveiling feel like?

_____

_____

_____

_____

_____

_____

_____

_____

_____

_____

_____

_____

_____

_____

_____

_____

_____

_____

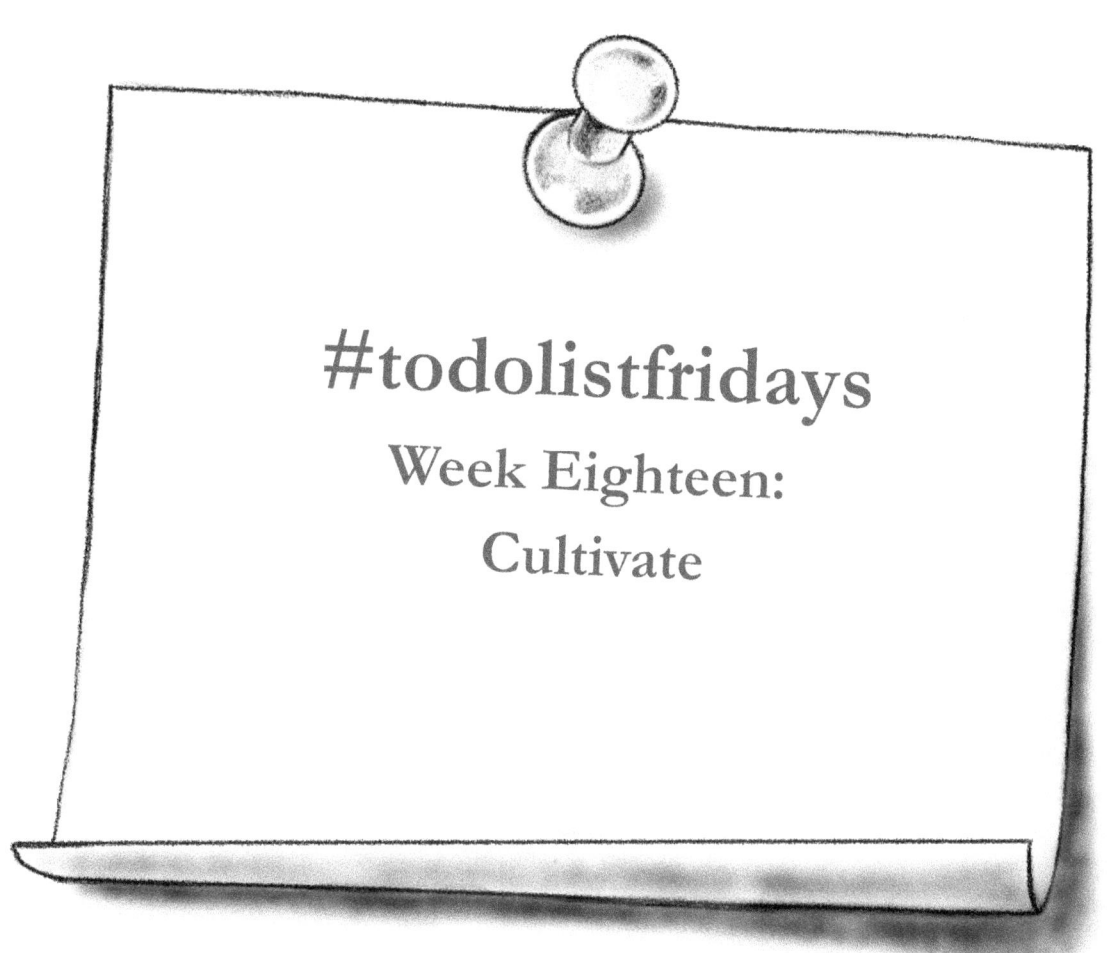

#todolistfridays

Week Eighteen:
Cultivate

It could be just another Friday, or it could be the day we begin cultivating . . .

An **EXPECTANT** heart — one that is always open to the possibility that something good will happen in our life;

An **ATTENTIVE** heart — one that is sensitive to the world around us at all times and constantly on the look-out for "clues" that are intended to point us in the direction of the realization of our innermost dreams and desires;

An **ADAPTIVE** heart — one that is willing to embrace a path and/or a desire that we might not initially have considered, but, due to a change in heart or circumstance, takes on a special meaning in our life;

A **PROACTIVE** heart — one that is committed to passionately pursuing all that is good;

A **GRATEFUL** heart — one that begins each day in search of something or someone it is grateful for;

A **PATIENT** heart — one that appreciates the truth of the timeless adage that good things take time; and

A **GIVING** heart — one that realizes that, at the end of the day, our true beauty, our sense of self-worth, and the fullness of our life is determined not by how we look, what we possess or how we compare, physically or otherwise, to others, but rather by the extent to which we empty ourselves in serving others.

Imagine having a heart like that.

HERE'S A SECRET: You already do!

You just lost sight of it "for a minute" in all the "adulting" you're running around doing.

An Invitation to
Reflect & Respond

When was the last time you genuinely EXPECTED something good to happen? If that kind of hope has been in short supply, what might be getting in the way? What's one thing you can do this week to begin nurturing an expectant heart again? Try and remember a change in circumstances that rerouted your life in a way you didn't plan—but are now grateful for? What did that look like and what would it look like to more freely embrace an adaptive heart today? What is one small, daily practice you could begin this week to awaken or reawaken a grateful heart? What does a giving heart look like in your life right now? What's one way you could quietly "empty yourself" this week in service, support, or encouragement of someone else? Which of these seven heart postures feels most familiar to you right now? Which one feels most foreign—or forgotten? What would it mean to believe that it's still in you, just waiting to be reawakened?

_____

_____

_____

_____

_____

_____

_____

_____

_____

_____

_____

_____

_____

_____

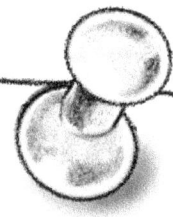

#todolistfridays

Week Nineteen:
Give the Gift that Keeps on
Giving – the Gift of Being
Noticed

If you're like me, chances are there are days when you WISH you were invisible.

Days when the worker bee in you is being pulled in a hundred different directions, by a hundred different people – most of whom know little about the pieces of you that matter and, aside from your ability to produce, to create, to problem solve, really don't care to.

Days when you can't bear the thought of doing one more thing for one more person or, worse yet, the thought of disappointing them by not doing it, when you can barely muster the energy needed to get out of your own bed, let alone find the reserves required to motivate others to fight their way out of theirs.

Days when you'd like to just to hit the pause button and give you and your weary heart a little time and space to breathe, when you want to isolate, when you long for nothing but silence, when the introvert in you would prefer to have no human contact at all.

Days when you want to leave The Cape hanging in the closet and just be Clark Kent, when you need to take a break from adulting and spend a little time being a child, when you just want to lace up a pair of tennis shoes and head out on a walk or grab a towel and be soothed by the sound of ocean waves lapping up the shore.

Days when, if you're to be honest, you just want to run away - from ALL of it.

But has there ever been a time when, despite wanting to be seen, to be noticed, without having to take the initiative, without having to set yourself on fire, you actually FELT invisible - unseen, overlooked, insignificant, or, worse yet, expendable?

I've tasted that feeling more than once, and I can tell you, without equivocation, it's pretty hard to swallow. I can't even imagine having it for breakfast, lunch, and dinner every day as I fear too many in the world – in our worlds – do.

The GOOD NEWS is: By paying a little closer attention, dispelling the notion that "they just want to be left alone" (trust me: no one does), and not leaving the noticing, acknowledging, appreciating, and affirming to someone else, we can all play a role in the fight against invisibility and the loneliness that accompanies it.

And we must, because if my brief encounters with invisibility are fairly representative, where this adversary is concerned, the line between FEELING you're invisible and BELIEVING it is a lot finer and more dangerous than we think. Let's do this!

An Invitation to
Reflect & Respond

Can you remember a time when you felt unseen, unacknowledged, or like your presence didn't matter? What made you feel that way? What did you long for in that moment? Are there areas of your life where you intentionally downplay your needs or emotions because it feels safer to stay invisible? What's the cost of doing that over time? Can you recall a moment when someone did notice you in a meaningful way—a passing compliment, a check-in, a glance that said "I see you"? How did it affect you? What's one intentional act you could take this week to make someone feel deeply seen—not for what they do, but for who they are? Sometimes we want to be noticed, but we send subtle signals that keep others at arm's length. What's one way you could let yourself be seen a little more clearly this week—with honesty, vulnerability, or simply openness?

_____

_____

_____

_____

_____

_____

_____

_____

_____

_____

_____

_____

_____

_____

_____

_____

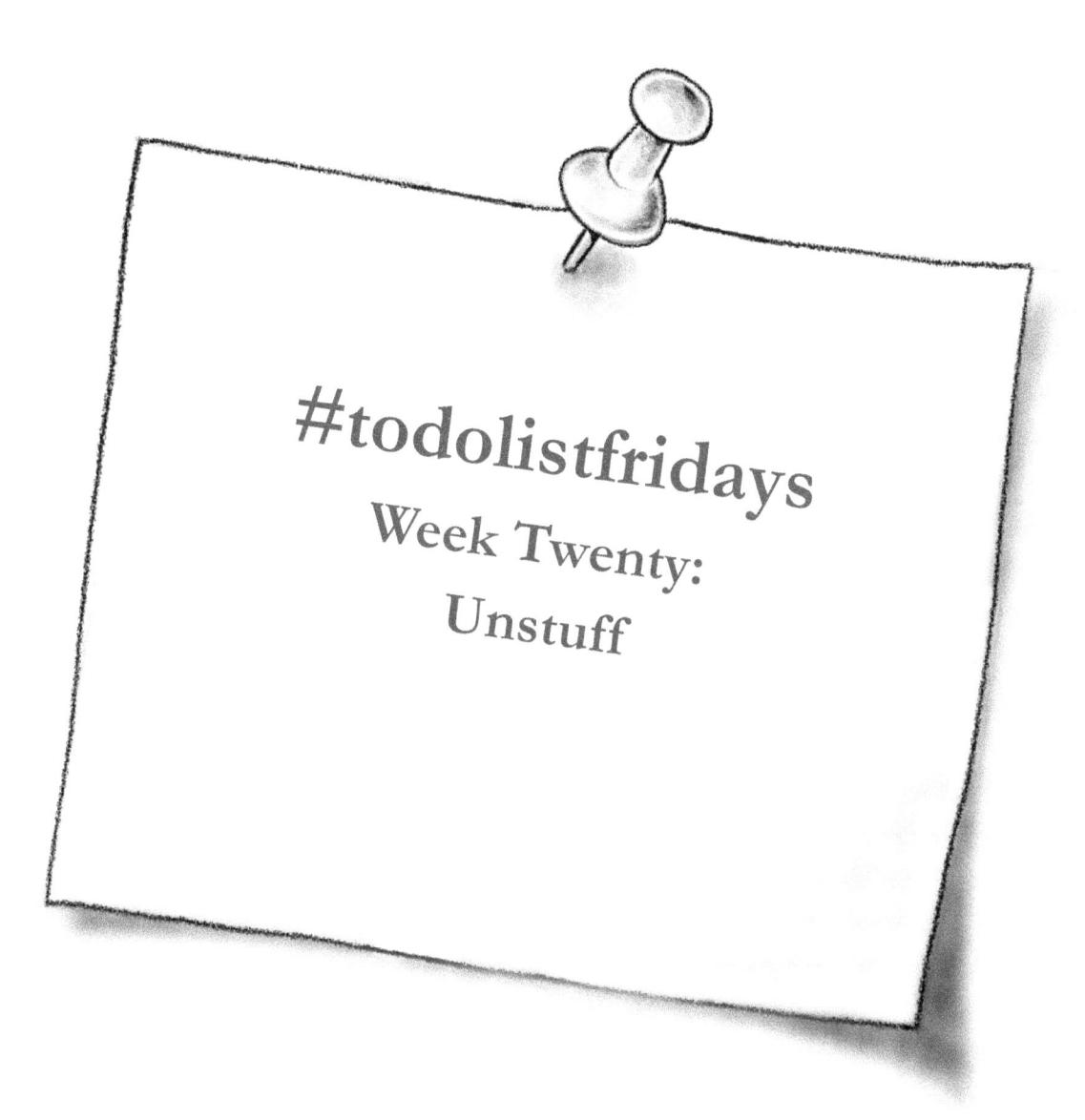

#todolistfridays
Week Twenty:
Unstuff

Our family's ability to accumulate and hold onto STUFF is legendary – at least in my mind. In fact, during a recent move, I managed to fill 92 U-Haul boxes – of every conceivable shape and size – with STUFF. I then promptly transported all that STUFF to what is now not one, but two large storage units, so that it could join 50 other boxes of STUFF from a prior move that I could tell were growing very lonely as a result of our not having even visited, let alone opened them for the better part of two years.

Don't get me wrong. Our family's unparalleled skill in collecting STUFF is not something I'm proud of. In fact, quite the opposite. Over time, I've actually grown to detest STUFF. Why? Because I've learned the hard way that STUFF gets in the way of things – important things. It also consumes valuable time – time that could be spent fostering healthy human relationships, communication, and connection.

Worse yet, STUFF distracts us from the need to be present, from noticing and paying closer attention to things that are hiding in plain sight. As if that were not reason enough – and, believe me, it is - STUFF has to be tended to. You have to organize it, find space for it, fix it, maintain it, clean it – and, once you get attached to it (which you inevitably will), you have to cart STUFF around with you wherever you go. And when the day comes when you are no longer around, someone else has to tend to your STUFF, sell it, sort it, or start the process of dragging it around with them and their STUFF all over again.

A few years ago, I got so disgusted with STUFF that I sat down with a piece of paper and tried to figure out what STUFF I actually NEEDED to live my life. This is the list I came up with: a bed, a pillow, a couch, a desk, a computer, a bathroom, a kitchen, a T.V. (to watch The Masters), a cup, a plate, a set of utensils, a few changes of clothes (and a place to put them), a pair or two of shoes, a car, and the few odds and ends that go along with those things, but only one of each.

Why then did I spend so much of my life feeling so claustrophobic in my own living spaces? Why was there always a veritable tsunami of STUFF everywhere I looked? Where did all that STUFF come from? What possessed me to think I needed even a fraction of it? Who was I trying to impress with all the STUFF and why? Most importantly, why didn't I jettison it years ago, so that I could have room to breathe, to think, to not be distracted, to live unencumbered, to focus on what matters?

I've long wanted a simpler, less STUFF-filled life. I only wish it hadn't taken me as long as it did to act on that want.

An Invitation to
Reflect & Respond

Take a moment to consider: What kinds of stuff are cluttering your life right now? It might be physical possessions—but could also be "noise," emotional baggage, toxic relationships, unrealistic expectations, or overcommitments. How does all that "stuff" make you feel—overwhelmed, anxious, stuck, resentful, exhausted? What would your life feel like with less? Why do you think you've held onto certain things—objects, ideas, roles, relationships, or routines—that no longer serve you? What fear, identity, or image have they been helping you preserve? If you made a "What I truly need" list or your own, what would be on it? What's one small piece of "stuff"—tangible or intangible—you can let go of this week? Something that no longer reflects who you are or where you want to go?

_____

_____

_____

_____

_____

_____

_____

_____

_____

_____

_____

_____

_____

_____

_____

_____

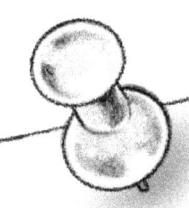

#todolistfridays
Week Twenty-One:
Stop Trying to Squeeze
Boundless Love Into Little
Boxes.

Several years ago, I sat down for dinner with a therapist friend at a conference in the Midwest. We'd been corresponding for months via social media, but, because we lived thousands of miles apart, had never met in person.

Within minutes, my heart told me that its counterpart across the table was very special and, for the next two hours, my friend and I "got out of their way" and just let the two of them talk to one another. It was as if they'd known each other since birth.

A few years later, I received a break-of-dawn text. My friend had suffered an unspeakably traumatic family tragedy – one I felt completely ill-equipped to respond to. Late one night, in the midst of her overwhelming grief, I texted simply, "If it's any comfort, know this. I love you and have since the day we met. There, I said it!"

Her response caught me a bit off guard, "What kind of love are 'we' talking about? Care to expand?" In retrospect, her question shouldn't have surprised me. After all, I too had long since grown accustomed to fitting LOVE into not-so-neat little, "worldly-appropriate" boxes (romantic, parental, familial, friend, etc.) and to receiving and expressing it accordingly. The world insists we do that virtually from the moment we dip our little toe into the muddy waters of adulting.

You'll find my "reply" to my friend's text in one of the most powerful pieces in my book, **Retune Your Heart**. For now, I offer this:

Macie doesn't love that way. She spends EVERY WAKING MOMENT loving EVERYONE whole and open-heartedly—and, I might add, apologizes to NO ONE for her indiscriminance. She also receives love with the same reckless, peddle-to-the-metal abandon. And here's the thing. Every heart that is lucky to be showered or even sprinkled with a droplet of that love is immeasurably brighter, lighter, and more joyful because of it.

"What kind of love am I talking about?" The REAL kind. The BOUNDLESS kind that accompanied all of us into this world. The SOUL DEEP kind. The TETHERED AT THE HEART kind. The kind that was never meant to and never will fit into a box.

An Invitation to
Reflect & Respond

Growing up, what messages did you receive about how love should be expressed, categorized, or contained? How have those messages shaped the way you give and receive love today? Have you ever experienced love that didn't fit neatly into one of society's "acceptable" boxes? How did it feel to try to name or define it? What might have changed if you simply let it be? Think of someone in your life with whom you share a deep, soul-rooted connection. If you were to describe that love without using conventional labels (friend, partner, sibling, etc.), what would it sound like? What words would you use? Think of someone in your life with whom you share a deep, soul-rooted connection. If you were to describe that love without using conventional labels (friend, partner, sibling, etc.), what would it sound like? What words would you use? What fears or hesitations come up when you think about offering boundless love in your life—without condition, without labels, without apology? What might be possible if you did it anyway?

_____

_____

_____

_____

_____

_____

_____

_____

_____

_____

_____

_____

_____

#todolistfridays

Week Twenty-Two:
Steal Home

Those who are old enough to remember may recall Charles Shulz's "Peanuts" comic strip. In one especially iconic edition, the reader is offered a glimpse into the thought processes of the strip's main character, Charlie Brown, a kind-hearted, but highly-indecisive and insecure boy, who finds himself "trapped" between his desire to be "the GOAT" and his fear of being "the goat."

The choice seems simple enough. Does he risk stealing home and potentially realize his dream of being the hero of the game or stay glued to third base where there is no risk - save that of spending the rest of his life wondering "what could've been"? It's a dilemma all of us confront at one time or another in Life – it and the flood of "what if" questions that invariably accompany it.

Regrettably, like Charlie, we too often allow FEAR to not only frame but answer those questions – "What if it doesn't work out?" "What if I fail? "What if I embarrass myself?" "What if I'm not _____ enough?" I know because I spent A LOT of years on third base. Eventually, however, I came to realize that there are a whole host of other "what if" questions that are far healthier and more life-affirming that we could – and, I humbly suggest, should - be asking ourselves.

Here are just a few that come to mind:

What if today you decided to just show up, that you are enough – just as you are?

What if today you lived like those who know you best and love you most have been right all along – that you are courageous, resilient, and worthy?

What if today you came out of the shadows, stood in the light, and allowed yourself to be seen as you are – uniquely beautiful?

What if today you believed that "you" actually are worth living for, worth fighting for – worth going the extra mile for?

What if today you resolved that enough is enough – that you've beat yourself up enough, lived small long enough and are enough?

What if today you let love in?

What if today you loved "you" differently than yesterday – a little more tenderly, a little less critically, and a lot more generously?

What if today you focused on a singular goal: To reclaim and honor your authentic self?

What if today, instead of judgment, you finally offered your thirsting heart the forgiveness and grace it has been longing for?

What if today you turned the page on the story with the unhappy ending you've been telling yourself all these years and wrote a different one?

What if today is that day you replaced what you perceive as the certainty of a given outcome with the possibility of a different one?

Now you're ready! Go ahead. Steal home!

An Invitation to
Reflect & Respond

What is something you've been standing on the edge of doing for far too long—something you've dreamed of, but haven't moved toward? What's keeping you frozen in place (fear, self-doubt, the need to be perfect)? What's your version of Charlie Brown's "What if I fail?" narrative? What are the fears or false beliefs that whisper to you when you consider taking a risk? Choose one fear-based "what if" that's been holding you back. Now rewrite it into a more life-affirming version. For example: "What if I fail?" "What if I grow in ways I never imagined?" Think of someone who has seen the best in you—even when you couldn't see it in yourself. What would they say to you right now, as you inch off third base? If you were to "turn the page" and begin writing a new chapter of your life—one not ruled by fear but by possibility—what would be the first sentence? The first bold action?

_____

_____

_____

_____

_____

_____

_____

_____

_____

_____

_____

_____

_____

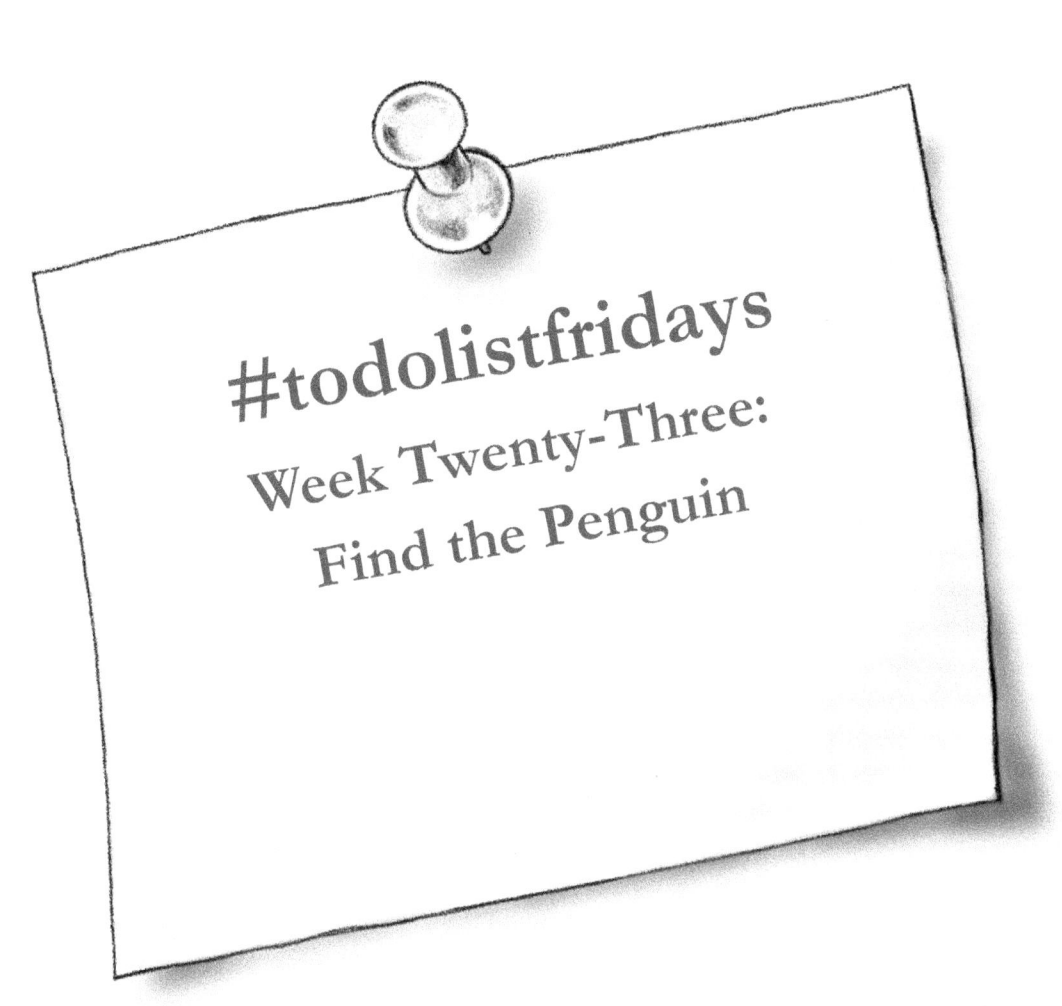

#todolistfridays
Week Twenty-Three:
Find the Penguin

It was 55 degrees at the park, borderline FRIGID by Florida standards, which prompted a puzzled then two-year-old Macie to ask: "Where are you snow?" "Penguin, where are you?"

Once upon a time, not so long ago, our unworldly-adorned, curiously-inquisitive, ever-expectant hearts asked those same questions even on "cold" gray days.

Now, we mostly complain about them – I know I do – and if we wonder at all it's not about where the penguins are hiding, but whether and when we'll see the sun again.

Make no mistake. It's a choice. And it's one we make 100's of times a day. But only one of the two choices holds the promise of a joyful heart.

So if joy is what you seek, the next time you're "offered" the choice between playing hide and seek with a penguin or boarding the train to Bitterville, take a page from **The Playbook of Your Childhood Heart**.

Find the penguin!

An Invitation to
Reflect & Respond

Think of a time when you could've reacted with frustration or cynicism, but instead chose to laugh, explore, or smile? What were the circumstances? What did that choice feel like? What ordinary things filled you with joy or wonder as a child? How many of them still show up in your day-to-day life? What might it take to invite one of them back? Commit to seeing every day this week through Macie's eyes. No matter what Life throws at you, search for and find "the Penguin." Write down what you notice and delight in. Is there a recurring complaint or negative narrative you've been holding onto lately? What would change if you paused and replaced criticism and cynicism with curiosity?

_____

_____

_____

_____

_____

_____

_____

_____

_____

_____

_____

_____

_____

_____

_____

_____

_____

_____

#todolistfridays

Week Twenty-Four:
Cling to Christmas

I don't know about you, but most of the adults in my world (yours truly included) can't put Christmas away fast enough. And, on some level, I get it. We've distorted the holiday in ways that have stripped it of its magic and made it too much like work.

Truth is, we adults seem to have a penchant for doing that with A LOT of things that were meant to be light, pure, playful, celebratory, spontaneous, unencumbered, and organic (e.g., relationships, social gatherings, vacations, parenting, Life, etc.). We overcomplicate them, contaminate them, clutter them, and, in the process, slowly siphon the joy out of them.

But, Macie takes a VERY DIFFERENT approach. She's in no hurry for Christmas to end. In fact, for her, every morning IS Christmas morning. That's because, unlike us, Macie hasn't learned to take Life for granted.

She also doesn't live in fear of the uncertainty that is an inescapable part of a new day. Quite the opposite. She can't wait to blast out of her crib and embrace it – ALL of it. In fact, like a beautifully-wrapped present under the tree, it's precisely the uncertainty of what might unfold before her - combined with her insatiable curiosity - that holds the magic.

All of which got me to thinking. What if instead of greeting the new day and its inevitable uncertainties with an expectation of "sameness" or, worse yet, trepidation, we too treated it like Christmas morning, the way Macie does – the way all of us once did.

What if we channeled that same sense of wonder and curiosity that filled our hearts when we woke to find an exquisitely-wrapped gift under the tree with our name on it and allowed it to inspire and motivate us to get out of bed and embrace those uncertainties, rather than allowing them to be a paralyzing force in our lives.

What if, in short, we insisted that fear take a back seat to our childhood sense of adventure? What if I told you it's essential to our ever finding true JOY again? What then?

An Invitation to
Reflect & Respond

Can you remember a time when you woke up excited for what the day might bring—before your to-do list, your fears, or your responsibilities kicked in? What was different about that day? Why do you think we're so quick to "put away" things like Christmas, celebrations, or joy? What have you boxed up in your own life that might be longing to be let out again? What might help you look at each new day as a gift instead of a grind? What's something in your life right now that was once light, playful, or meaningful—but has started to feel heavy, overcomplicated, or joyless? How can it be simplified or reimagined? When you think about the uncertainty of tomorrow, what's your first emotional response—fear, dread, numbness? What might shift if you greeted it with curiosity instead?

_____

_____

_____

_____

_____

_____

_____

_____

_____

_____

_____

_____

_____

_____

#todolistfridays
Week Twenty-Five:
Rest

I know for many the prospect of facing a new day, let alone a new week or a new year carries with it a weight that seems almost unbearable, a sense of overwhelm and impossibility, a feeling of already having fought more than enough battles for one lifetime, an uncertainty in the ability to take even one more step – exhaustion.

But I also know this from having spent a season (or two) in those dark places - we are much stronger, more courageous, and more resilient than we realize.

We also have a greater capacity for patience than we ever imagined and, while in the moment it may not seem or feel like it, an uncanny ability and insatiable desire to overcome.

If today, this week, or this year find you among the many, I encourage you to draw strength from those truths.

And if, as I suspect, you've already gone the EXTRA MILE, I implore you to pause for a minute, a day – heck take an entire week - to rest and catch your breath. You've earned it.

Then keep going, keep fighting. keep loving, keep believing.

Because the magic you're searching for may well be in the next one!

An Invitation to
Reflect & Respond

What physical, emotional, or spiritual weight have you been quietly carrying for far too long? When was the last time you gave yourself permission to set it down, even for a moment? What is getting in the way of you doing that? Take a moment to reflect on all the battles you've already fought and survived that once seemed impossible? What does that say about your strength and resilience? What old messages or beliefs about hard work, self-worth, productivity, or "toughness" are keeping you from the soul-replenishing rest you so desperately need? What do you need to hear, from yourself or someone else, to allow yourself to really rest this week?

_____

_____

_____

_____

_____

_____

_____

_____

_____

_____

_____

_____

_____

_____

_____

_____

_____

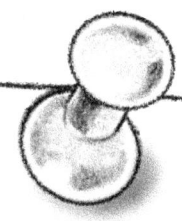

#todolistfridays

Week Twenty-Six:
When Offered the Choice Between
Adding to the Hurt or Contributing to
the Healing, Always Choose Healing.
P.S. You Always Have a Choice.

The heart is the most powerful and vital organ in the human body. It's also one of the most resilient. It can endure tremendous suffering and abuse and still find a way to recover.

But, even the heart has its limits. It can only be dismissed, disrespected, invalidated, diminished, disregarded, demeaned, criticized, insulted, bruised, and ignored so many times before it begins to shut down, to shut out, and, eventually, to turn away.

The thing is, too often, we lose sight of that truth and the fact that every angry, critical, hurtful, judgmental, and careless word, every vacuous, drive-by hug, every teardrop shed uncaught; every overture of love left unrequited; every insult, every act of indifference, insensitivity, rebellion, and abandonment; every moment spent unnoticed, unappreciated, and unpursued; and every turning and running away; brings the heart on the receiving end one incrementally small, invisible step closer to that limit.

I realize some hurt is unavoidable, an inevitable by-product of what it means to be fully human, fully alive, and fully engaged. But, so much of it is avoidable – and there's simply no more room for that kind of hurt in the world.

It's time to acknowledge that our hearts are super saturated with it.

It's time to dial it back, to check mean-spiritedness at the door – all the doors (*e.g.*, our homes, our offices, our churches, our playgrounds, our virtual portals, etc.) – and leave it there.

It's time to stop hurting and start healing.

It's time we gave a second or, in some cases, a first thought to the impact we – our words and our actions – are having on our own hearts, the hearts of others (colleagues, family, friends, and strangers alike), and our collective heart.

It's time we ask ourselves if we and they are adding to the hurt or contributing to healing. Because it's one or the other. There is no middle ground here.

We can all do better. We must do better. There's A LOT hanging in the balance.

An Invitation to
Reflect & Respond

When was the last time you were faced with the choice between healing and hurting—whether you realized it in the moment or not? Which did you choose and why? How might the situation been different if you chose healing or grace? Where or with whom have you grown emotionally careless with your words and actions? In what ways have you been dismissive, critical, hurtful, or invalidating toward yourself? How has your own unhealed hurt shaped the way you treat others? If hearts really do have limits, whose heart might be nearing its breaking point because of something you've said—or failed to say? Are you more invested in being "right" or being healing?

_____

_____

_____

_____

_____

_____

_____

_____

_____

_____

_____

_____

_____

_____

_____

_____

_____

#todolistfridays
Week Twenty-Seven:
Retire the Cape

Chances are if you're like most, somewhere between deftly responding to half a dozen break-of-dawn emails, fighting and, hopefully, winning the battle of blasting the kids out of bed, getting them clothed, fed, and off to school, taking the dog for a walk, cramming in a quick work-out, hurriedly putting yourself together, shoveling down a bite to eat, and racing out the door to begin tending to the mountain of Friday morning, afternoon, and early evening emergencies waiting for you at work, you've already managed to slip yours on today – as you likely have most days since first dipping your little toe in pool of "adulthood."

If so, you know a little something about the exhausting and often self-suffocating weight The Cape carries with it - the feeling that you need to be all things to all people all the time; the inability to say "no" to opportunities to swoop in and "save the day" no matter how overwhelmed you already are, the refusal to relinquish control and let others step in and step up, the constant placement of others' needs and wants above your own, the inevitable feelings of inadequacy it generates, and the real or perceived lack of room, let alone grace, for even the smallest of missteps or mistakes, in short for anything less than superhuman.

Turns out, there's a reason Superman and Superwoman have been relegated to fictional, indeed comic book, status: They're fun to imagine, but trying to emulate them in real life is no fun at all. It's actually quite unhealthy for all involved and, taken to an extreme, potentially life-threatening.

My suggestion? Do whatever is necessary and draw whatever boundaries need to be drawn to let it be known that, from here on out, "Clark" (and "Kristin") will be just fine thank you!

An Invitation to
Reflect & Respond

What are the responsibilities, roles, or expectations you carry every day that feel heroic in scale? How have they taken a toll on your body, emotions, or relationships? Can you remember when you first felt the need to "be everything to everyone"? What messages or experiences taught you that you had to earn love, safety, or belonging by doing it all? What makes it hard for you to say no? Is it fear of disappointing others, losing control, or appearing weak? What might be possible if you said "no" more often—not out of selfishness, but out of self-respect? What's one mistake or imperfection you've been beating yourself up over that you'd instantly forgive in someone else? Can you offer the same grace to yourself? What would it sound like if this week you wrote a resignation letter to your "cape-wearing" role? (*e.g.*, "I resign from the belief that I must _____. I am choosing _____ instead").

_____

_____

_____

_____

_____

_____

_____

_____

_____

_____

_____

_____

_____

_____

_____

_____

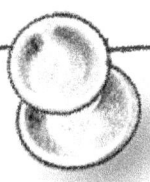

#todolistfridays

Week Twenty-Eight:
Devote 10 Percent of the Time
You Spend Focusing on AI to
Focusing on EI

I'm fascinated by our preoccupation with the approaching tsunami of Artificial Intelligence (AI).

Seems everywhere you turn these days there's another article, podcast, blog post, news segment, or water cooler conversation devoted to AI's seemingly limitless potential to fundamentally change virtually every aspect of our personal and professional lives – every aspect that is, but the piece that matters most and continues to receive the least attention: Our Emotional Intelligence (EI).

I'm told that I should be concerned about AI for lots of reasons – not the least of which is that's coming after my job! But, if I'm to be honest, my concerns about the impact AI may have in the future, even on my future, pale in comparison to the fear and broken heartedness I experience daily over the immeasurable damage that already has been and is being done by our individual and collective indifference to the gaping holes in our EI.

We continue to ignore those holes at our own peril, because, sooner or later, there will be a breaking point.

We simply can't keep treating each other with contempt, keep cavalierly hurling hurtful, poisonous, and divisive words at one another, keep pretending mental illness and the embarrassing lack of resources that exist to combat it are "someone else's problem," keep turning a blind eye and a deaf ear, rather than an open, empathetic heart to the real life struggles of others (family, friends, colleagues, and strangers alike) and expect there not to be profound consequences.

We can do better, friends.

We have to do better and we have to start now.

An Invitation to
Reflect & Respond

How much time and energy do you devote to AI? How does that compare to the time you spend working on your emotional self? In what ways do you use technology to avoid or bypass emotional interaction and discomfort (e.g., scrolling instead of processing, texting instead of calling, multitasking instead of listening)? How might be more fully present help restore connection? Try and recall a time when someone has shown you emotional intelligence—listening without judgment, offering grace, seeing your humanity—how did that affect you? What's one small way you could begin to "invest" in EI this week—either by building your own emotional skills or by tending more mindfully to the emotions of others?

_____

_____

_____

_____

_____

_____

_____

_____

_____

_____

_____

_____

_____

_____

_____

#todolistfridays
Week Twenty-Nine:
Be a Little Less and a Little More

Imagine what life would look like if we were just . . .

a little less critical and a little more compassionate
a little less judgmental and a little more empathetic
a little less harried and a little more patient
a little less distracted and a little more present
a little less bitter and a little more loving
a little less fearful and a little more adventurous
a little less wedded to perfection and a little more accepting and understanding of our
shared humanity
a little less clingy to the hurts others have inflicted and a little more forgiving
a little less bound up with misplaced shame and guilt and little more open to the gift of
grace
a little less preoccupied with the things we don't have and a little more grateful for all that
we do
a little less tethered to the missteps in our past and a little more focused on the next step
in the journey
a little less put together and a little more authentic
a little less walled off and a little more vulnerable.

I have and it's beautiful. It's also achievable.

An Invitation to
Reflect & Respond

Look through the contrasting pairs in this week's reflection. Which one speaks loudest to you right now? Why do you think that particular contrast touches a nerve—or brings hope? When you feel quick to judge someone (or yourself), what might it look like to pause and ask: What don't I know? What story might be unfolding beneath the surface? What shame or guilt are you still carrying that no longer serves you? What would it mean to open your heart—even just a little—to the idea that grace isn't something you earn, but something that's freely given and deserved? Choose one of the "less/more" pairs to focus on for the next seven days (*e.g.*, less fearful, more adventurous). What's one small way you can live that intention each day?

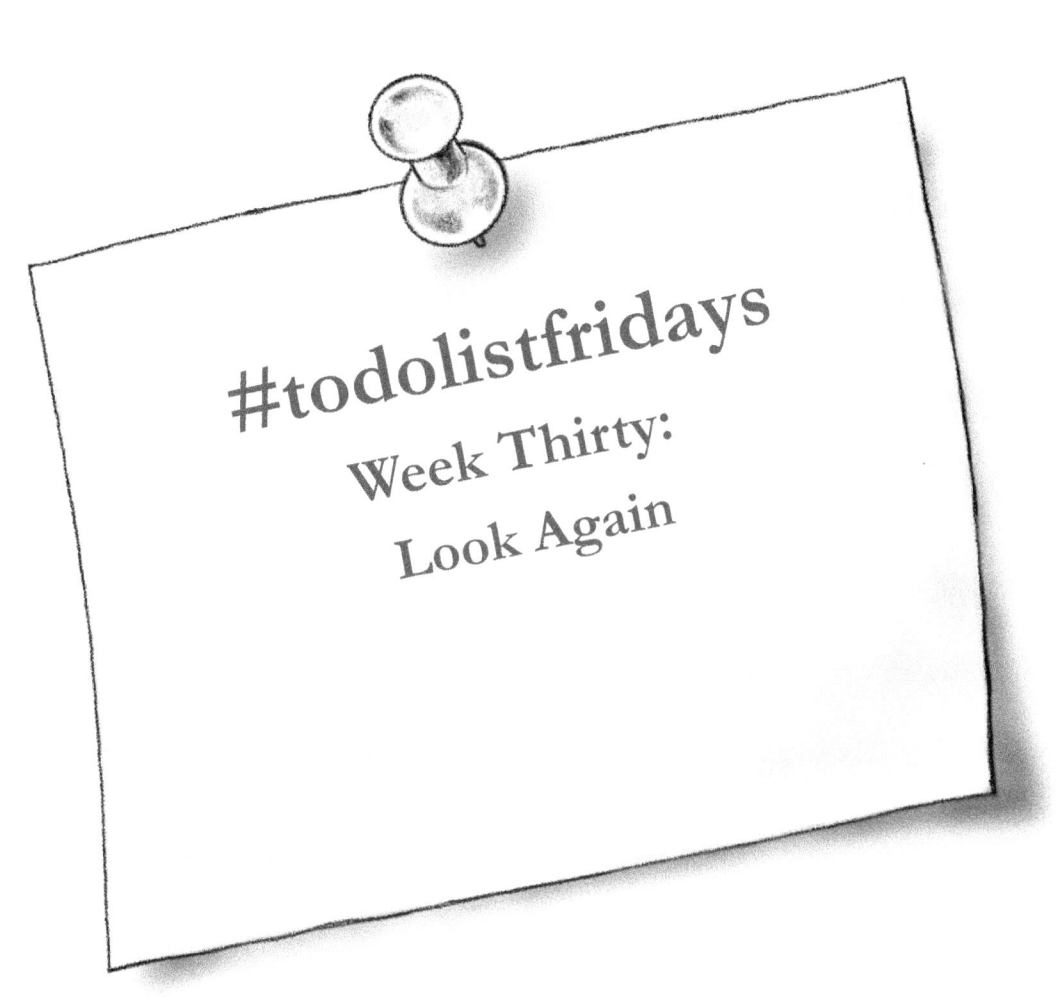

#todolistfridays
Week Thirty:
Look Again

We spend way too much time and expend way too much emotional capital searching for the truth about us – for the things that define us, make us worthy and desirable, set us apart - in all the wrong places, beginning with the mirrored reflection we see of ourselves first thing every morning.

Truth is: We will never find it there.

It lies instead in the reflections we create in the sometimes radiant, often tear-filled eyes of those whose lives we touch with gifts unique to each of us that will never be captured by a mirror – gifts of friendship, kindness, trust, compassion, empathy, encouragement, understanding – even the simple gift of our mere presence and our willingness to listen – to name just a few.

I've seen those reflections countless times in my life.

But, what's important to me is that YOU see them. Because, I promise: If you will embrace the inescapable reality that I know to be true about you, even though you and I have never met (*i.e.*, that you are not the person you perceive or misperceive yourself to be in the mirror any more than I am), you WILL see it – time and time again – and it may just change (or save) your life.

So, if, when you looked in your mirror of choice this morning, you didn't see strong, resilient, courageous, overcomer, bold, uniquely beautiful, cherished, and irreplaceable, I encourage you to look again and to keep looking until you see it, because it's there to be seen.

And if you're in a place right now where you can't trust your own eyes to see it "borrow" someone else's - someone you can trust, who knows you and loves you.

An Invitation to
Reflect & Respond

What do you usually look for when you look in the mirror—flaws, fear, or confirmation? What narratives have you silently accepted about yourself that may not be true? Whose voice do you hear when you criticize yourself? Where did it come from? If the mirror told the whole truth, what would it say that you've been refusing to hear? When was the last time someone reflected your goodness back to you? What parts of you are not reflected in a mirror but show up clearly in relationships? Write the name of one person who truly sees you. Ask them: "What do you see in me that I might not see in myself?"

_____

_____

_____

_____

_____

_____

_____

_____

_____

_____

_____

_____

_____

_____

_____

_____

_____

_____

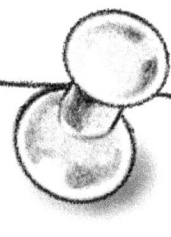

#todolistfridays
Week Thirty-One:
Be a Simon and Garfunkel
Kind of Bridge

Searching for the perfect gift to give that special someone?

Consider giving the promise found in these iconic lyrics - and then live it.

Come to think of it, why wait for a holiday, and why limit the giving of it to only the special?!?

"When you're weary, feeling small,

When tears are in your eyes, I will dry them all.

I'm on your side when times get rough and friends just can't be found.

Like a bridge over troubled water, I will lay me down.

When you're down and out. When you're on the street.

When evening falls so hard, I will comfort you.

I'll take your part when darkness comes and pain is all around.

Like a bridge over troubled water, I will lay me down."

Bridge Over Troubled Water, Simon & Garfunkel (1970)

An Invitation to
Reflect & Respond

Who has been a "bridge" for you when it mattered most? Have you told them what their presence meant to you? Is there someone in your life right now who may be weary, down, or hurting? What would it look like for you to "lay yourself down" for them? What keeps you from stepping in when others are struggling? Is it fear, lack of time, discomfort, uncertainty about what to do or say? What would happen if you showed up anyway? What might it mean to be that for someone else, even in a small way? This week, consider this question: "Where might a bridge be needed — and how might I become it?"

#todolistfridays

Week Thirty-Two:
Come Up for Air

I can't tell you how many times I've sat down in a bar or restaurant over the years and found myself sitting near someone (I admit it's usually a guy!) who didn't STOP TALKING long enough to take a breath from the moment I sat down until the moment I left.

I don't know if it's a genetic thing, an ego thing, or a function of our (men) having a uniquely inappropriate relationship with the sound of our own voice.

But I know this: (1) I'm pretty sure, once upon a time, I was "that guy;" and (2) it's not good for lots of reasons.

For starters, it leaves no room for others to share things that actually matter – like matters of the heart.

Second, even when others do manage to get a word in edgewise, our eagerness to jump back in makes it IMPOSSIBLE to LISTEN – and, increasingly, the art of listening is EVERYTHING.

But fear not, we can do better, and we must.

Here's a "simple" homework assignment to help. This weekend, if you find yourself out at dinner or a social event, check the "being the life of the party" role at the door and, instead, be the one who listens and pays careful attention to others' words and hearts.

Be open to telling others who may be surprised by and inquire about your "quietness" that you're conducting a social experiment of sorts. You might even encourage others to share.

Then, open your ears and heart wide and LISTEN – attentively. Trust me, it'll be a game-changer. I promise.

An Invitation to
Reflect & Respond

Think of a recent conversation where you may have done more talking than listening. How might that exchange have shifted if you'd chosen to pause and truly listen instead? When was the last time someone really listened to you — not to respond, but to understand? How did that make you feel? In what ways might "coming up for air" — slowing down your speech, your reactions, your presence — create space for deeper connection with others? Is there someone in your life you sense may need to be heard? How could you intentionally create that space for them this week? What might change in your relationships if you approached conversations as a learner, rather than a storyteller?

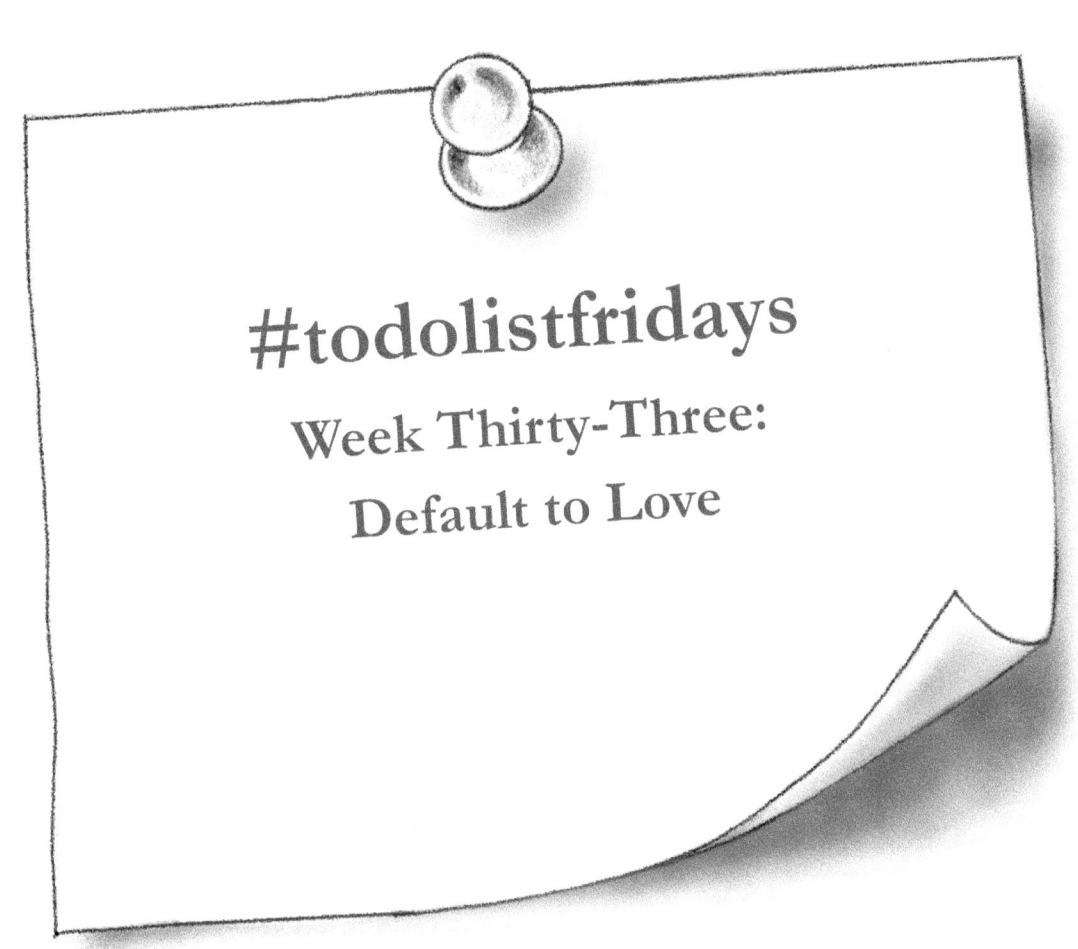

#todolistfridays

Week Thirty-Three:

Default to Love

Imagine what your world, the worlds of those you interact with, especially those you profess to care about most, and the world at large would look like if the next time your heart was triggered to respond with anger, bitterness, resentment, or hate, you defaulted instead to LOVE.

And not just a lame, drive-by, "said-'I-love-you'-a-million-times-so-clearly-I-do" kind of love. No. I'm talking about

- a feel it in your bones kind of love
- a steadfast, not going anywhere (other than by your side) – ever – kind of love
- a pick you up, dust you off, and carry you on my back to safety kind of love
- a four-legged friend kind of love
- a constant, unwavering, and unconditional kind of love
- a predictable as the sunrise, reliable, patient kind of love
- a desirous of understanding kind of love
- a slow to criticize, let alone judge kind of love
- a childlike, honest, transparent kind of love
- a "your burdens, brokenness, and pain are mine too" kind of love
- a "together we'll work whatever it is out" kind of love
- a "you are never alone" kind of love
- an any hour of the day or night my heart is open for business kind of love
- a given freely with no strings attached kind of love
- a willing to get messy kind of love
- a run into a burning building kind of love
- a guide you home kind of love.

I know it sounds impossible. I also know it's not. Difficult? Yes. Undoable? No. Capable of being done perfectly? Not a chance.

Worth doing however imperfectly? Absolutely!

Truth is, once upon a time, we all loved like that. We've just forgotten how. It's time we start remembering.

An Invitation to
Reflect & Respond

Think of a recent moment when you reacted with frustration, impatience, or judgment. What might have changed in that moment if you had paused and responded with love instead? Which of the descriptions of love from this week's message resonate most deeply with you? Why? Who in your life needs to hear or feel that "kind of love" from you right now? How will you let them know? Imagine what it would look like for you to re-learn how to love like a child—freely, fully, and without expectation? Reflect on the people who have shown you "run into a burning building" kind of love. How did that change you? How can you honor that love this week? What practices daily, spiritual, or relational practices might help you default to love more often?

_____

_____

_____

_____

_____

_____

_____

_____

_____

_____

_____

_____

_____

_____

_____

_____

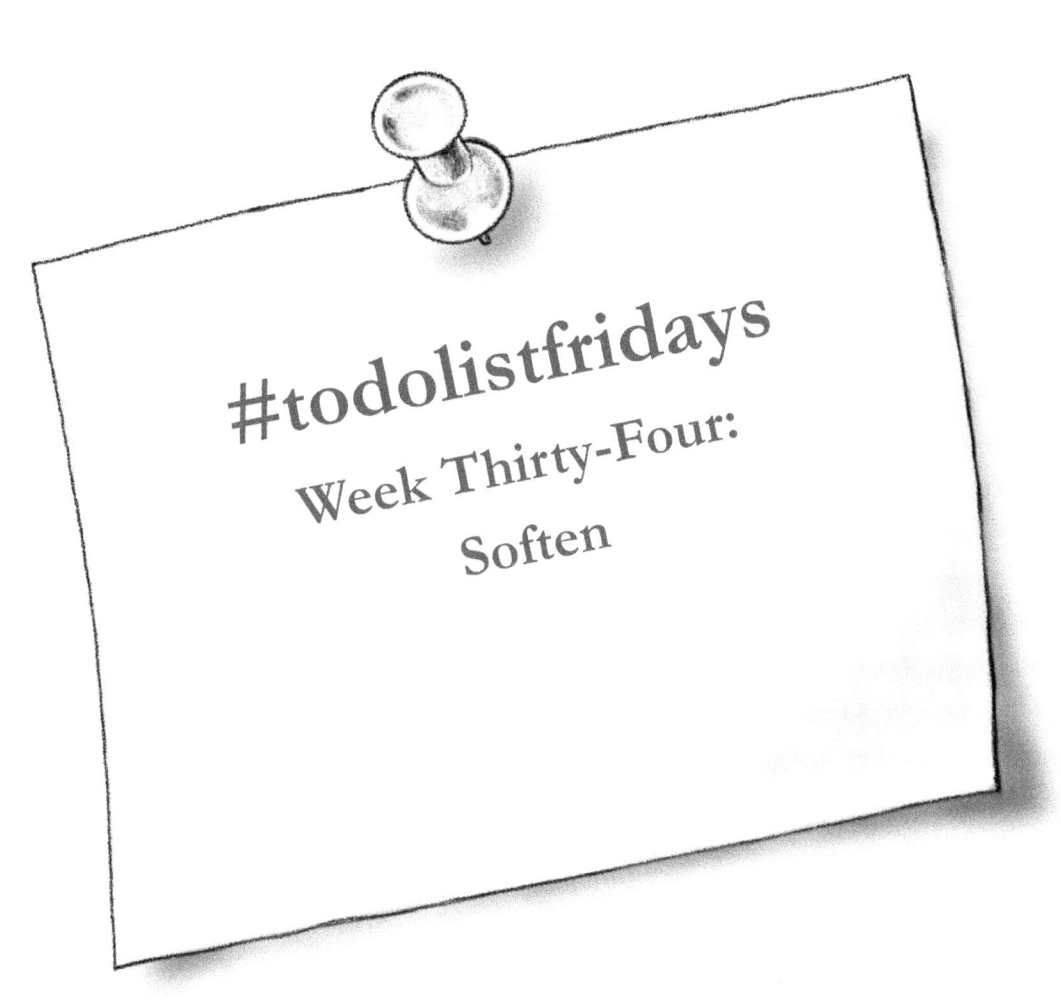

#todolistfridays
Week Thirty-Four:
Soften

Somewhere along the way, we got the idea that to not only survive, but thrive in today's business and professional worlds we'd need hard edges, leather tough skin, and a titanium shell around our heart.

I believe the opposite is true: that being truly successful in both our professional and personal lives requires just as much softness as it does steel - if not more.

What does that look like?

It looks like ego taking a back seat to humility, seeming invincibility to vulnerability, and judgment to empathy and compassion.

It looks like acknowledging our own, sometimes sizeable mistakes, imperfections, and human frailties before, if not in lieu of, repeatedly accosting others with the smallest of theirs.

Trust me: The last thing the world needs right now is harder hearts. What it needs are softer ones.

I know I do.

An Invitation to
Reflect & Respond

Reflect on where you have grown emotionally hard without realizing it? What pain might be hiding underneath that toughness? When was the last time you allowed yourself to be tender—allowed someone to see beyond your hard outer shell? What are you most afraid would happen if you allowed yourself to be a little softer? What positive changes could come with softening? Consider whether the hard edges are serving you. How would your life and the lives of those you love look and feel if you allowed yourself to be a little more vulnerable and, in the process, gave them permission to be vulnerable in return?

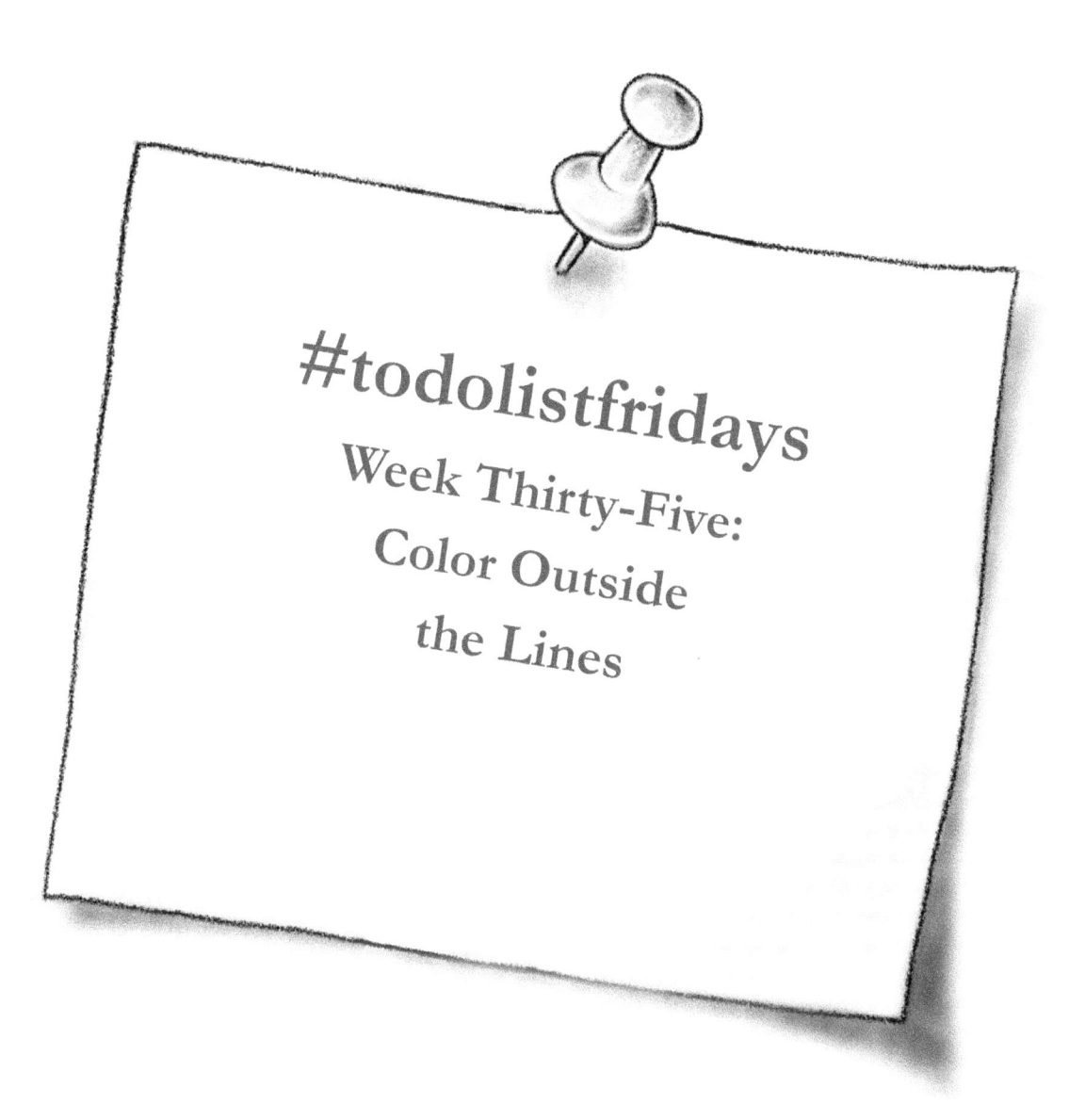

#todolistfridays
Week Thirty-Five:
Color Outside
the Lines

Dear Macie,

Make no mistake.

There will come a time when the world will want, expect, even insist that you "color within the lines."

It will ask you to squeeze into one of its too-narrow, very adult boxes, temper your expressions of self, and stifle your creativity.

Politely decline the "invitation."

Take risks.

Live full. Love hard. Be you!

Love,

Papa Don

An Invitation to

Reflect & Respond

When was the last time you let your imagination run wild without worrying about judgment, structure, or expectations? What did it look and feel like? Are there any "boxes" you've allowed yourself to be put in that no longer fit who you are or want to become? What "lines" were drawn for you growing up — by others or by yourself? Who drew them and how did they serve either you or the drawer? If you gave yourself full permission to break through or at least explore "coloring" outside one "line" in service of joy, self-expression, or growth, what would it be? Imagine writing a letter to your younger self — or a child you love — encouraging them to stay true to their voice. What would it say?

_____

_____

_____

_____

_____

_____

_____

_____

_____

_____

_____

_____

_____

_____

_____

_____

#todolistfridays

Week Thirty-Six:
Commit to Removing
One Brick

Anyone who's ever broken a bone that required casting knows the speed with which our muscles atrophy with non-use.

But, last night, it occurred to me that OUR HEART – the most powerful and important muscle in our body – is equally susceptible to that same phenomenon.

Why then do so many of us insist on building brick (or, in some cases, titanium) walls around it, masking it, using substances and other unhealthy behaviors to try and numb it, and, in the process, deprive it of the "exercise" it needs to remain strong?

I'm not talking about a 5-mile run or walk, a grueling CrossFit session, or another Spin, Kickboxing, or Pilates class. I'm talking about REAL EXERCISE, the kind that can only come from experiencing the full range of emotions it was so beautifully designed to handle - love, hope, joy, sadness, passion, acceptance, rejection, empathy, disappointment, frustration, fear, loss, gratitude – to name just a few.

Want to give your heart the workout it's been thirsting for since the day most of us first set foot in adulthood?

Commit to removing just one brick this week, resisting the urge to reach for your numbing agent of choice the next time uncomfortable emotions starting flooding in, and allowing yourself (and your heart) instead to remember what it's like to FEEL IT ALL – the way you (all of us) once did.

Believe me, the more "repetitions" you do the stronger you (and your heart) will get. I promise.

An Invitation to
Reflect & Respond

When did the walls start going up around your heart and why? What purpose did constructing those walls serve in the moment? What the "cost" of constructing and maintaining? Do they still serve you? Can you recall a time when you allowed yourself to feel it all? How did your heart respond in the moment—and after? What might removing "one brick" a day look like for you this wee? Could it be a conversation, a confession, a quiet moment, or simply withholding the usual numbing response? How could embracing vulnerability—even temporarily—open you to deeper connection, growth, or healing?

_____

_____

_____

_____

_____

_____

_____

_____

_____

_____

_____

_____

_____

_____

_____

_____

_____

_____

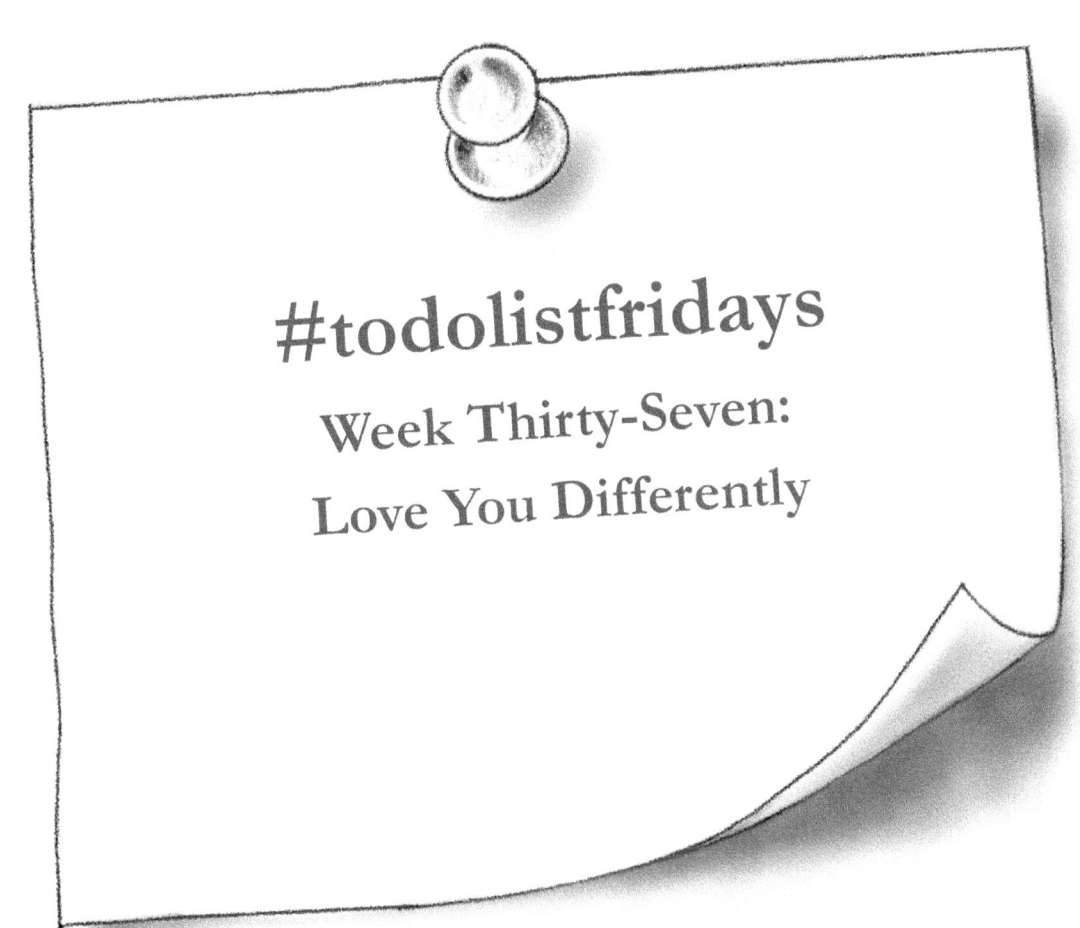

#todolistfridays

Week Thirty-Seven:
Love You Differently

Lots of people may have gotten it wrong where loving you is concerned …

discouraged, when what was needed was encouragement;

judged, when a little bit of understanding would've gone a long way;

turned a deaf ear, when all you wanted was to be heard;

demeaned, when your already guilt and shame-filled heart thirsted for affirmation;

offered a cold shoulder, when what your weary soul longed for was a warm embrace;

harshly criticized, when compassion and empathy were the soothing balm you sought;

shut you out, when you desperately needed to be invited in;

clung to past missteps, when forgiveness was what you hoped for;

been blind, when your pain was in plain sight …

But you don't have to be one of them!

You can love "you" differently – compassionately, tenderly, non-judgmentally, empathetically – the way you've always wanted to be loved, deserve to be loved, were created to be loved, and are worthy of being loved.

And, you can speak to "you" differently - with words that encourage, that affirm, that forgive, that are kind and gentle – that give credit where credit is due.

Because the truth is: The best way to show others how you long to be loved is to live and love "you" that way.

So, why not start this weekend. Heck, why not start right now, by pausing for just a moment to consider what "loving you" looks like?

Maybe loving you is . . .

a warm candle-lit bath,
a quiet afternoon with a favorite book,
a night out (or in) with your favorite meal,
a pen and a blank sheet of paper,
snuggles with your four legged friend,
a day's respite from an artificial number on a scale,
playing hooky and picnicking at your special place,
a long drive to nowhere in particular with the wind in your hair and a favorite song on the
radio,
time spent with favorite photographs,
a "to do" list (or two!) – not this one of course! - torn to shreds, a smile in the morning
mirror,
a whispered word of affirmation,
a cup of coffee with a friend you've been meaning to reconnect with.

Do that this week. Practice loving you – unapologetically.

An Invitation to
Reflect & Respond

In what ways have others "gotten it wrong" when it comes to loving you? Which of those moments still live quietly in your heart? What words or actions hurt the most—and why? Where have you learned to speak to yourself the way others once spoke to you? How would you speak to yourself if you truly believed you were worthy of love? What really restores you? What would feel like kindness to your soul right now? If you could give yourself one gift this weekend, what would it be?

_____

_____

_____

_____

_____

_____

_____

_____

_____

_____

_____

_____

_____

_____

_____

_____

_____

_____

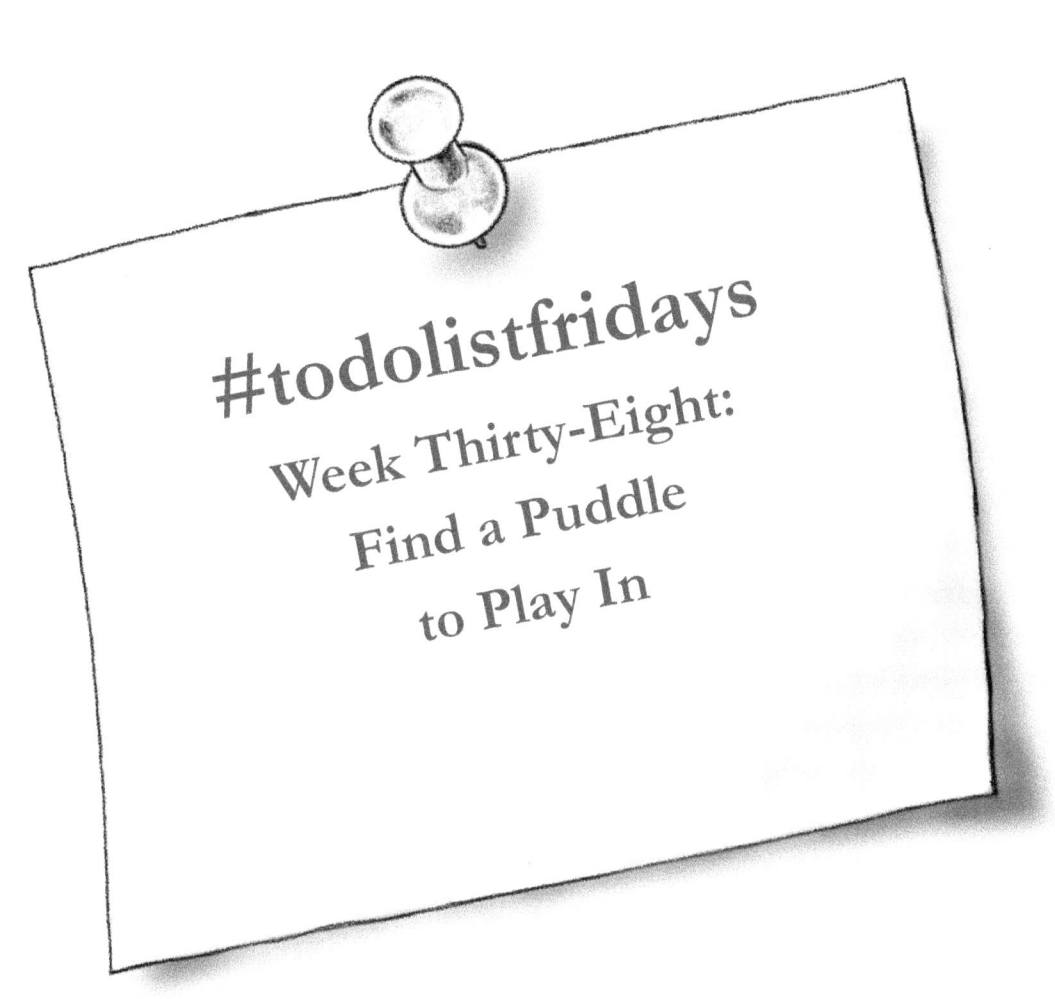

#todolistfridays

Week Thirty-Eight:
Find a Puddle
to Play In

I can't remember the last time I played in a puddle, let alone decided to "wash my hair" in one and came out with pieces of mulch stuck to my face.

But Macie did all three the other day and had THE TIME OF HER LIFE!

I'm also not sure when I decided to jettison my own childlike sense of playfulness and spontaneity from my VERY ADULT daily routine.

But I know this - as unconscious as I'm sure it was, it was a REALLY BAD decision.

I'm not suggesting we run out, find the nearest puddle, and dance around in it until we're soaked to the bone, though I confess, at times, the thought of doing that has more than a little appeal to me.

I am, however, convinced that all of us would benefit from taking ourselves, our work, and how "put together" we insist on APPEARING to the rest of the world a little less seriously and creating a little more space for play.

Maybe this weekend we can find a way to test the theory!

An Invitation to
Reflect & Respond

What did play look like for you as a child? When was the last time you felt genuinely silly, spontaneous, or joyfully messy without caring who was watching? Think about a moment when you let your guard down and truly embraced play. What would it take for you to allow yourself that freedom again, even for a moment? Who is a playful friend or colleague you could you invite on this personal "social experiment" of yours? This week, consider ways—small or big—that you can invite play back into your life. How might that shift your perspective, your mood, or even your relationships?

_____

_____

_____

_____

_____

_____

_____

_____

_____

_____

_____

_____

_____

_____

_____

_____

_____

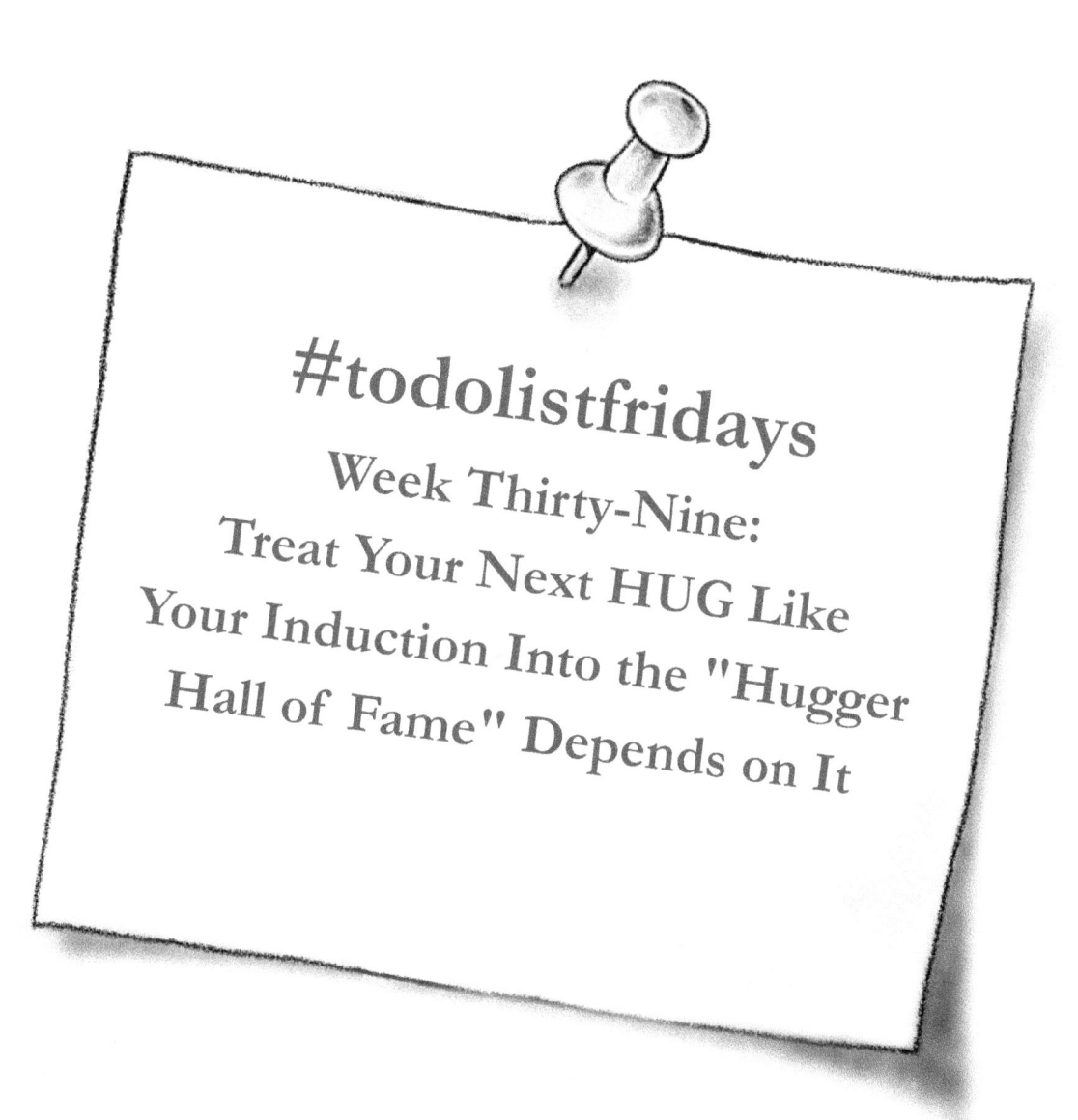

#todolistfridays
Week Thirty-Nine:
Treat Your Next HUG Like
Your Induction Into the "Hugger
Hall of Fame" Depends on It

I've never met a human being, who, at the end of a long and stressful day, wouldn't benefit from a hug.

I'm not talking about a lame, drive-by hug.

I'm talking about a REAL one - a hug that says, "you matter to me," "I value you for who you are – not what you do," "you are not alone," "you are not defined by whatever misstep you may have made today," "there is no need for perfect here," "my life is better because you're in it," etc.

Truth is, I don't know any human being whose heart wouldn't benefit from a hug like that at any time of the day or night.

And, it turns out there's science to back me up on that (Just Google "The Science of Hugs"). The bad news is, there just aren't enough hugs like that in the world.

The good news is: We all have the capacity to change that! Take it from someone who used to suck at hugging, it's an acquired skill and one well worth perfecting!

An Invitation to

Reflect & Respond

When was the last time you received a hug that felt like it spoke directly to your heart? What made it so meaningful? Think about someone in your life right now who might need that kind of hug. What's stopping you from giving it to them? How do you usually express comfort or love to those close to you? Are hugs part of your emotional vocabulary? In what ways might offering more intentional, wholehearted hugs deepen your relationships—with others and with yourself? What would it take for you to become a more present, heart-forward hugger, even if it feels a little awkward at first?

_____

_____

_____

_____

_____

_____

_____

_____

_____

_____

_____

_____

_____

_____

_____

_____

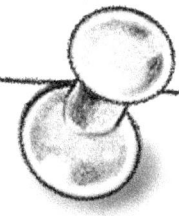

#todolistfridays

Week Forty:
Send a Word Hug. It Might Just
Change (or Save) a Life

Dear Macie,

Your physical beauty is beyond description.

But it's the parts of you no mirror will ever capture that are most beautiful to me - the joy in your heart, your tender, but feisty spirit, your quiet disposition, the many faces of your quirky and engaging personality, and your boundless energy and curiosity.

You have a warmth and calmness about you that are contagious and soul-soothing, a fierce sense of determination, a laugh that lights up a room, a seemingly insatiable desire to share closeness, and a "snugglability" factor that is off the charts.

Too soon, the world will try its best to convince you otherwise, to make you believe there are missing or misfitting "pieces" of your acoustic, uniquely beautiful self, that you need a little more of this or a little less of that to be enough, to fit in, to be accepted.

The world is wrong.

Don't be misled.

Wrap yourself instead in this word hug, cling to the truth about you - and just be unapologetically, unabashedly you!

Love,

Papa Don

An Invitation to
Reflect & Respond

Who in your life could use a heartfelt reminder of how deeply valued, seen, and loved they are right now? Have you ever received a "word hug" — a message or note that left you feeling truly known? Who sent it? What were the circumstances? What did it change for you? What truths about your acoustic, uniquely beautiful self have been buried beneath the world's noise? What would it take to begin reclaiming them? Make it a point to look in the mirror in the coming week and speak (or write) a truth to yourself that a younger version of you needed to hear — and still does. Begin building a habit of verbal affirmation: once a week, reach out to a loved one with words that uplift, affirm, or celebrate them.

_____

_____

_____

_____

_____

_____

_____

_____

_____

_____

_____

_____

_____

_____

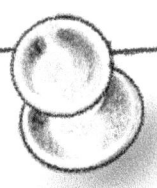

#todolistfridays

Week Forty-One:
Find Your Way
Back to the Playground

There was a time – not so long ago – when a twig, a leaf, and an empty playground on a sun-kissed September morning was all it took to evoke joy like they evoke in Macie in you and me!

It was a simpler, more innocent, quieter time.

We were above and undistracted by the noise.

We were lighter, unburdened by the weight of the world, of life, of work, of flawed relationships, and of an overwhelming sense of responsibility - for everyone and everything but ourselves.

We had an unobstructed view of self – not one obscured, if not entirely distorted by others, by comparison, or by our own self-loathing.

We (and our hearts) were free to live in and express our acoustic/authentic selves without fear of criticism, abandonment, or exclusion.

We were exactly who we were made to be and experienced life exactly the way we were intended to – with curiously, wonder, excitement, and awe. We were adventurous and fearless in all the right ways.

The challenge – for all of us – is to find our way back to that playground and rediscover our own twigs and leaves – and the joy and beauty to be found in the simplest of things.

Thank you, Macie for constantly reminding me of what we left behind and what's waiting for us when we find our way back.

An Invitation to
Reflect & Respond

When was the last time you experienced pure, uncomplicated joy? What were you doing—and what made it so joyful? What simple things did you once treasure as a child that you've since forgotten or dismissed? How has the noisiness of life—responsibilities, relationships, or self-doubt—hampered your ability to find and experience joy? In what ways have your efforts to avoid sadness, anxiety, or pain also impeded your ability to feel joy? Identify one way you treat "revisit" the playground of your childhood free from the weight of comparison, perfectionism, or over-responsibility. Write it down and commit to honoring it this week.

_____

_____

_____

_____

_____

_____

_____

_____

_____

_____

_____

_____

_____

_____

_____

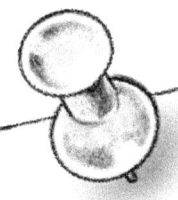

#todolistfridays

Week Forty-Two:
Forgive as if Your Heart Health
Depends on It, Because It Does

I don't fully understand why, as adults, we have the difficulty we do FORGIVING. Maybe we're delusional.

Maybe, in our ego-centricity, we've actually managed to convince ourselves that, unlike every other HUMAN who has ever set foot on the planet, we have never and would never hurt someone the way someone has hurt us.

Maybe it's all about anger and our very HUMAN desire for retribution – a desire fed by the wildly mistaken belief that our non-forgiveness is actually a burden borne by the unforgiven.

Maybe we believe that, by forgiving, we are somehow condoning or excusing the behavior that gave rise to the need for forgiveness and, in doing so, conferring a "win" on the wrongdoer.

Whatever the reason(s), I know this with absolute certainty, none are worth the emotional, psychological, and often physical toll failing to forgive takes on the non-forgiver.

I was twice-reminded of that in two separate conversations with two deeply-wounded hearts in just the last ten days.

The thing is: We didn't come into this world reluctant to forgive.

Quite the opposite actually. In fact, if you spend any time with a child, you not only will see the ease and frequency with which they forgive, but their penchant for reflexively handing out Second Chance Coupons to the mistake-maker, regardless of whether the insult to their personhood is large or small.

You and I once did that too, because, as children, we intuitively understood two things that we seem to have lost sight of on the road to adulthood.

First, that there's nothing to be gained from carrying the weight of non-forgiveness a moment longer than you have to.

Second, that, because we're HUMAN, sooner or later ALL OF US are going to do something profoundly hurtful to someone else and need - long for – forgiveness ourselves. Maybe it's time we revisit both of those inescapable truths.

And this one: When it comes to forgiveness, we can do better and, for the sake of our collective mental and emotional well-being, we need to do better.

An Invitation to
Reflect & Respond

When was the last time you withheld forgiveness? What emotions fueled that decision — anger, pride, fear, a sense of justice? Reflect on the cost of carrying that burden. Has it impacted your peace, your energy, your ability to connect with others, or even your physical health? Think back to your younger self — the child who gave out second chances freely. What would it take for you to return to that space of grace? This week, identify one person (even if it's yourself) toward whom you're holding resentment or unresolved hurt. Ask yourself: "Is continuing to carry this weight bringing me closer to the person I want to be — or pulling me further away?"

_____

_____

_____

_____

_____

_____

_____

_____

_____

_____

_____

_____

_____

_____

_____

_____

_____

#todolistfridays
Week Forty-Three:
Don't Let Joy Out
of Your Sight

In the lyrics to her hauntingly beautiful and troublingly relatable hit, "What Was I Made For," singer/songwriter Billie Eilish laments,

"I think I forgot how to be happy. Something I'm not. Something I can be. Something I wait for. Something I'm made for."

I don't know about you, but I've allowed myself to lose sight of JOY far too often in my life.

It's easy to do amidst the noise, when you're preoccupied with adulting, when you are (or believe you're) uber important, when you take yourself way too seriously - get mired in the "doing" rather than the living and the loving.

The thing is the more times you lose sight of JOY, the harder it gets to find it again. You forget where to look for it, what it feels like – how important it is.

Some eventually stop looking, decide it's just not worth the effort, that they "weren't meant to be happy," resign themselves to a life devoid of it.

My dad did that. Don't be that person.

If you're in a season where you've lost sight of JOY, take up the search. Try to remember where you found it the last time it went missing. Start there.

And, if you're still struggling to find it, consider looking where I most often do - in the heart of a little child, because JOY tends to go where it knows it's always welcomed.

An Invitation to
Reflect & Respond

Have there been times in your life when joy felt distant or unattainable? What were the circumstances? Can you recall a specific memory when joy was effortless and abundant? What made it possible in that moment? What are some patterns, responsibilities, or thought habits that have distracted you from experiencing joy recently? When you hear Billie Eilish's words — "I think I forgot how to be happy…" — do they resonate with you? Why or why not? What does joy mean to you now, and how has your understanding of it evolved since childhood? Make a short list of "joy triggers" from your past. Post it where you can see it daily and intentionally pursue one item from that list this week.

#todolistfridays

Week Forty-Four:

Just Live Today

Just live today.

Sounds simple enough. But what does that look like?

If we were 4 years-old (and, believe it or not, we once were!) it would look like living each day like we didn't have a past and didn't give a second's thought to the future.

Because all we knew and all we (rightly) cared about was what or who happened to be in front of us in any given moment – and making the most of it. We were fully present.

But something happened on the road to adulthood. Somewhere along the way, we picked up a hitchhiker known only as The Past – a surly character filled with missteps, guilt, regret, misplaced anger, shame, loss, hurt, brokenness, disillusionment, and disappointment - who refused (and still refuses) to get out of our car, so we cart him around with us.

And, we worry about the future – A LOT.

For us then, it looks like the emotional equivalent of a tax holiday. A day we don't have to add on. A moment of grace. A conscious EXHALE, where we give ourselves permission to let go of it all – the past, the future, the often soul-splintering weight of both – and just live today, just love today, just spend a day being FULLY PRESENT to whatever or whoever happens to be right in front of us.

What does "just living today" look like? It looks like allowing ourselves to be 4 years-old again for a day.

Trust me, while you may have forgotten what that looks and feels like, your heart hasn't.

An Invitation to

Reflect & Respond

When was the last time you truly lived in a day—not through it, past it, or around it, but in it? Reflect on how much of your emotional energy is spent reliving things you cannot change or bracing for things that haven't yet happened (and may never)? What would happen if you gave yourself permission to step out of that constant tug-of-war with your past and your future—for one day and just be fully present in the here and now? What small steps can you take this week to be more fully present to the people you're with, to the conversations you're having, to the moment you're experiencing?

_____

_____

_____

_____

_____

_____

_____

_____

_____

_____

_____

_____

_____

_____

_____

_____

_____

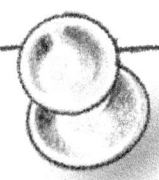

#todolistfridays

Week Forty-Five:
Be the Reason for
Someone Else's Smile

In case you're wondering. You didn't miss anything; that's it! Move on to the next page and accept the invitation to reflect and respond.

An Invitation to
Reflect & Respond

Who are the people in your life most in need of a smile today? What's stopping you from being a catalyst for someone's joy? Is it time, self-doubt, busyness, emotional fatigue? What would it take to push through that? Are you more comfortable receiving joy than giving it? Reflect on the role generosity (of spirit, attention, or kindness) have played in your life and relationships through the years. When was the last time someone said, "I really needed that" after a moment you created? What did you do, and how can you repeat or build on that? What can you do this week to be the reason for someone else's smile?

_____

_____

_____

_____

_____

_____

_____

_____

_____

_____

_____

_____

_____

_____

_____

_____

_____

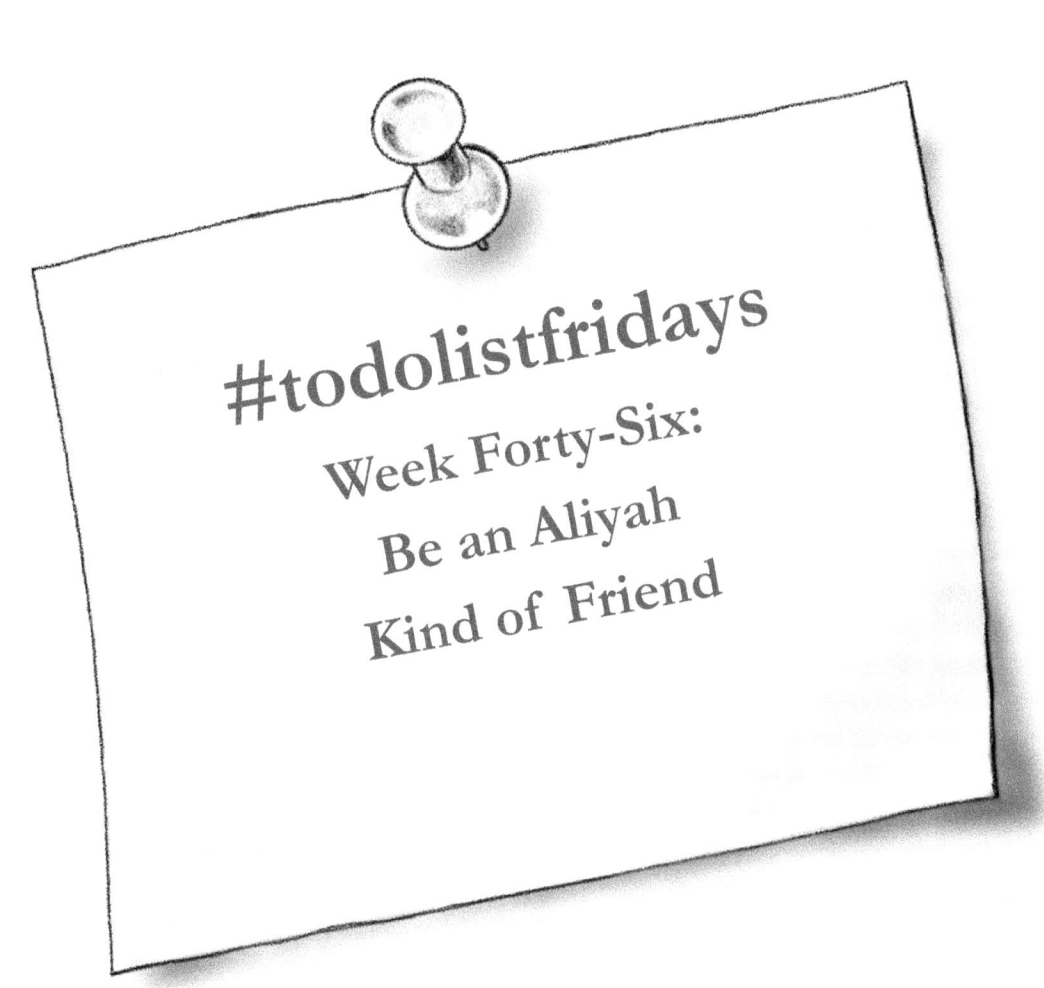

#todolistfridays
Week Forty-Six:
Be an Aliyah
Kind of Friend

Last year, I visited my grandson, Jake in Kansas to celebrate his 9th birthday and, as I walked through the door, he and his best friend, Aliyah greeted me.

While I'd heard a lot about Aliyah over the past few years, she and I had never met, nor had I ever had the privilege of seeing her and Jake together.

But, that weekend, I had a front row seat to the two of them for much of the two days we all spent celebrating Jake and I was captivated by what I witnessed, because it was immediately apparent to my heart that they were teaching a master class on what friendship, in its purest form, is meant to look, feel, and sound like and I was all in.

Yes, Aliyah is a classmate, playmate, and Lego-mate. Like Jake, she is bright beyond her years, quirky, and makes the Energizer Bunny look sloth-like. But, where Jake is concerned, Aliyah listens carefully and patiently, is interested in what he thinks, and curious about why he thinks the way he does.

She is also kind, soft, thoughtful, encouraging, and empathetic – in her words and actions – because she understands that Jake shares her sensitivity, and she cares (deeply and protectively) about his feelings.

She is engaged and attentive – and they never tire of each other. In fact, when they have to say goodbye, there is a subtle sense of sadness, as there should be.

Aliyah is a difference-maker in Jake's life – and he in hers. And, it's not because someone taught them how to be an extraordinary friend. It's because their hearts – our hearts – yearn for connection like that and intuitively know where to find and how to nurture it.

As I headed back to the airport early Monday morning and reflected on my visit, I wondered why Jake and Aliyah's friendship had touched me as profoundly as it did. Why, more than once, I caught a tear (or two) slipping down the sides of my face.

Part of it likely was my realizing how much I would have given up to have had a friend like Aliyah when I was 9 years-old and already far more familiar with loneliness than any 9-year-old should be.

But another part – the bigger, more beautiful part – no doubt stemmed from the realization that we all have the capacity to be and be the beneficiaries of an Aliyah kind of friend.

Imagine that. Now imagine acting on it. I did – and I smiled all the way back to Miami!

An Invitation to
Reflect & Respond

Recall a time when you experienced true, unconditional friendship. What qualities made that relationship feel safe, nurturing, or life-giving? Who in your current life would describe your "Aliyah"? What do the two of you do that makes each of you feel truly seen, heard, or valued? When was the last time you approached a friendship with wonder, patience, and genuine curiosity, like a child discovering someone for the first time? Reflect on your childhood friendships. Was there an "Aliyah" in your life when you were younger? Or were you that kind of friend to someone else? How does that memory make you feel now? This week make it a point to send a handwritten note to a special someone, expressing the impact they've had on you as a friend.

_____

_____

_____

_____

_____

_____

_____

_____

_____

_____

_____

_____

_____

_____

#todolistfridays
Week Forty-Seven:
Surprise Someone

There are very few people on the planet who prompt me to get up at 3:00 a.m. on a Saturday and drive 200 miles just to surprise them when they arrive at their beat-the-heat visit to the park. But Macie is one of them. And several weekends ago I did just that.

I only wish the whole world could've seen the smile that broke across her face like a sunrise breaking across the horizon when she first caught a glimpse of me, because, if they could have, they would understand the heart impact that awaits the giver and recipient of the gift of a surprise visit.

Chances are there's someone in your life right now whose heart would dance at the unexpected sight of you, the sound of your voice, or an unsolicited invitation from you to "come out and play."

Maybe it's an old friend or former colleague you've fallen a bit out of touch with, a parent, sibling, or relative you've been promising to make time for, or just someone you sense could use a reminder that they're cherished, missed, and worthy of the sacrifices involved with paying them a surprise visit.

I can assure you, based on very recent experience, it'll be well worth the effort - for both of you!

An Invitation to
Reflect & Respond

When was the last time you were truly surprised—in a good way? How did it feel? What about that experience made it so memorable? Think of someone in your life who might be quietly longing to feel seen, remembered, or loved. What has kept you from reaching out? What would it mean for you—and for them—if you bridged that distance? What holds you back from spontaneous acts of love or kindness? Pick one person—just one— and plan a small, heartfelt surprise this week: a handwritten note, an unexpected phone call, a meal delivered, or a spontaneous visit. Reflect on how the surprise made you feel. Did it shift your energy, your heart space, or your outlook for the day?

_____

_____

_____

_____

_____

_____

_____

_____

_____

_____

_____

_____

_____

_____

_____

_____

_____

#todolistfridays
Week Forty-Eight:
Look a Little
Closer

Do you see it?

The gift.

The hope.

The turned page.

The open door.

Yesterday (all of your yesterdays - heck the last 5 minutes) in the rearview mirror.

The offer of a second (or third) chance.

The seedling of a new beginning.

The cracking open of a treasure chest of possibilities.

The next word in your comeback story waiting to be written.

Another opportunity to love and be loved - to forgive and be forgiven.

A moment's peace.

The first or next step on the road to recovery.

It's more than just another sunrise, 24 more hours you have to "make it through."

It's an invitation.

It's the precipice of redemption.

It's what grace looks like.

A new day.

An Invitation to
Reflect & Respond

What gifts or invitations might be hidden in today that you've overlooked because you're focused on surviving rather than noticing? When was the last time you truly paused to acknowledge the grace embedded in a new day? Which of your yesterday's still hold too much of your attention? What does "the first sentence of next word in your comeback story" look like? If today was the turning point in your personal redemption arc, what would you choose to do with it? Take a picture of something beautiful or surprising you notice today — something you would have missed if you hadn't looked a little closer. Make one decision today that aligns with who you're becoming, not who you've been.

_____

_____

_____

_____

_____

_____

_____

_____

_____

_____

_____

_____

_____

_____

_____

_____

#todolistfridays

Week Forty-Nine:

Show Up

Several weeks ago, when I had nothing but time on my hands, I accepted an invitation from my friend, Sondra Kronberg, to be a guest on a Saturday morning online support group that she started at the advent of COVID for those battling and in recovery from eating disorders.

It's an incredible free resource and the "Morningside Chats in the Living Room" community is an extraordinary group comprised of some of the most uniquely beautiful, creative, courageous, and authentic human beings you could ever hope to meet. I love them.

The thing is, my life turned upside down in those intervening weeks - a move, a new job, a tiny apartment, two projects due the day of the meet-up today, and another due the following Monday. I had no time to prepare my remarks as I customarily do and I could feel the anxiety of it all starting to build.

Given the circumstances, Sondra would've understood if I told her I needed to reschedule. But, there's no way on Earth I was going to do that. "This group has had enough people 'not show up' for them through the years," I thought to myself. "I'm not about to add my name to that list. The 'right' words will come, but, even if they don't, I will - and that matters."

Sometimes we think "just showing up" is "the least we can do." I'm here to tell you that often it's all and exactly what someone needs us to do - because it lets them know they matter, that there's someone in their corner, someone who is FOR them, who believes in them, who is holding hope for them, someone who cares enough to show up.

"I can be that someone," I resolved, and later that day I was. My message: "Trading the 'What?' for the 'Why?' When Life Throws You A Curveball."

An Invitation to
Reflect & Respond

Recall a time in your life when someone simply showing up made all the difference. How did it impact you? Who in your world today might be quietly hoping for someone to show up for them? How often do you dismiss your presence as not enough? What if it's exactly what's needed? What does it say about us that we so often undervalue the quiet, consistent act of being present? How does your perception of "preparedness" get in the way of your participation or presence? Call, text, or stop by to connect with someone who might be feeling unseen. Don't overthink it—just show up. Commit to sitting beside someone in silence, being near them in stillness, or offering a listening ear without needing to fix or solve.

_____

_____

_____

_____

_____

_____

_____

_____

_____

_____

_____

_____

_____

_____

_____

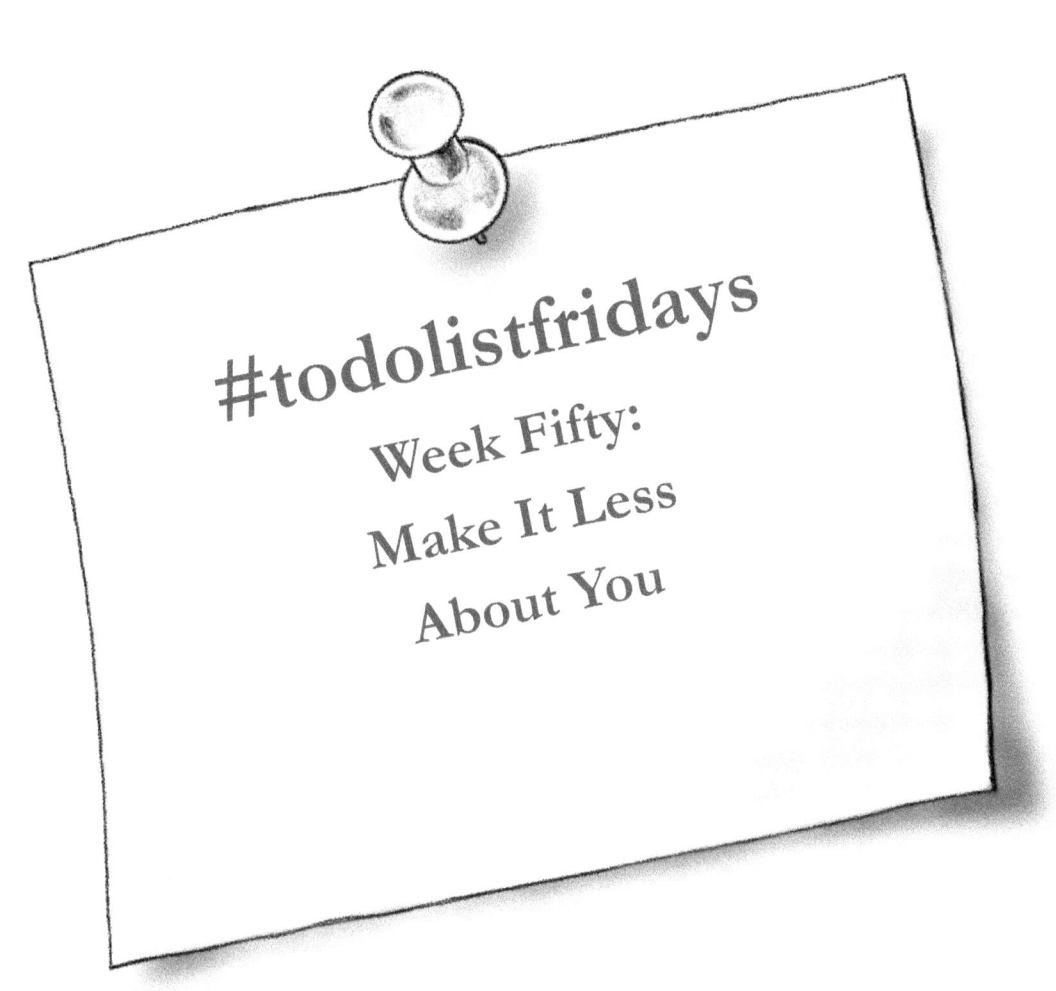

#todolistfridays

Week Fifty:
Make It Less
About You

"What's the IT?" you ask. Everything.

An Invitation to

Reflect & Respond

What would change in your life — in your relationships, your work, your conversations, your community — if you approached each day as though everything wasn't ultimately about you? What if the "win" wasn't being seen, but seeing someone else? What if the goal wasn't to be heard, but to listen intently? What if your presence was less about being impressive and more about being helpful? Where might you need to step back so someone else can step forward? Today, choose one area where your instinct is to take the spotlight — and consciously give it away. Offer genuine encouragement without needing acknowledgment. Do an anonymous act of kindness. Choose silence when you'd normally dominate the conversation.

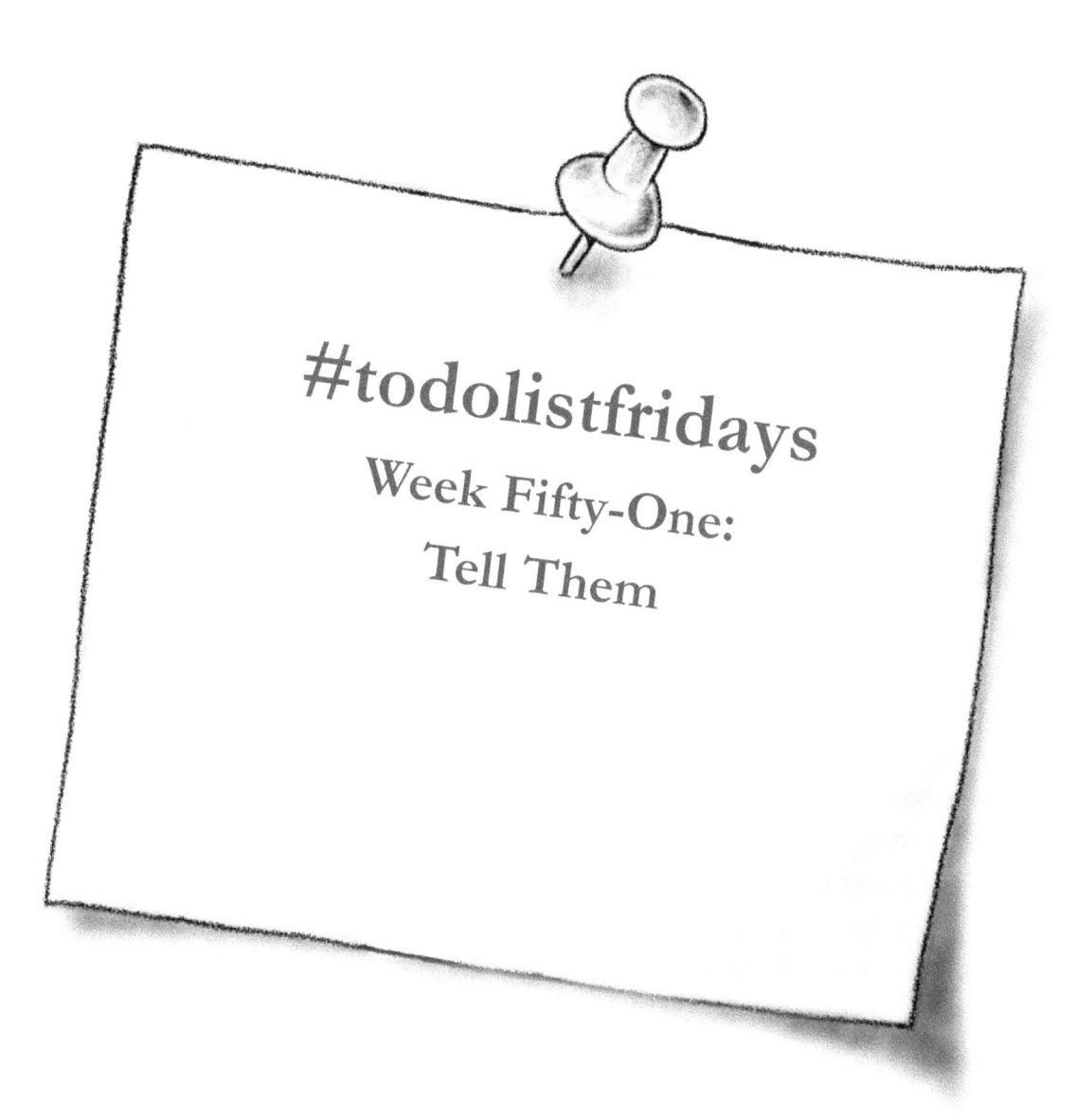

#todolistfridays
Week Fifty-One:
Tell Them

Don't assume the people/person in your life who matter/matters most know that they're not alone, that you're FOR them, that you VALUE them above all others, that you BELIEVE in them (unconditionally), and that you are and will be THERE for them - day or night, through thick and thin.

Because when the darkness and the doubt find their way to our doorsteps, as they inevitably, repeatedly, and often quite unexpectedly will, it's easy to lose sight of the truth about ourselves, of our worthiness and critically important to know that there's someone out there willing, eager to remind us. It only takes a moment to make a difference.

I encourage you to do it today - and, when I say "today," I mean like now.

An Invitation to
Reflect & Respond

Is there someone in your life who may not realize how deeply you care for or believe in them? When was the last time you told the people who matter most just how much they mean to you—not in passing, but with intention and clarity? What assumptions have you been making about how well others understand your feelings toward them? Are you willing to challenge those assumptions? If someone you love was struggling silently today, would they know that you're in their corner—without a doubt? Make it a habit. Set a recurring reminder—weekly or monthly—to reach out to someone important and tell them what you admire, love, or appreciate about them.

_____

_____

_____

_____

_____

_____

_____

_____

_____

_____

_____

_____

_____

_____

_____

_____

_____

_____

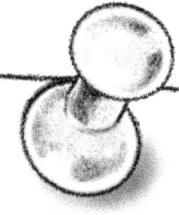

#todolistfridays

Week Fifty-Two:
Give Your Friends and Loved Ones the
Priceless Gift of Knowing that Where
You're Concerned Forgiveness for a
Lifetime is a Given

I don't know about you, but I feel like I've apologized enough for two lifetimes.

At one time or another, I've "apologized" for just about everything you can imagine - for being late and being too early, for not trying hard enough and trying too hard, for having to impose on another's time and not reaching out sooner, for not being a good friend and caring too much, for "should've-known-betters" and "wish-I'd-known-betters," for things I said and things I wish I had.

Heck, sometimes I've even felt the need to apologize for who I am, for my "differentness," my imperfections, for tears I've shed or caused others to shed, and for missed opportunities - some of which I didn't even realize existed. Imagine that. And I can't begin to tell you some of the apologies I've received through the years from family, dear friends, and strangers who had no business apologizing to me given all that they were dealing or trying to deal with in their lives.

Enough!

A few months back, I decided on a different approach. If you're a friend or family member and you "apologize" to me for acts or omissions that simply make you human, you get this note: "Please take your 'sorry' back. From this moment on, there will be no more 'I'm sorry's' exchanged between us. EVER. I've exhausted my quota for one lifetime (two actually) and, if this note is any indication, you have too.

Let's just assume from here on out that we're going to run out of time, fall short, be imperfect, and do God knows what else where each other are concerned a million times.

You're good by me. Apologies accepted in advance. And please, do me and you a favor. Don't ever apologize for being all that you are (INSERT LIST OF AMAZING TRAITS RECIPIENT ALWAYS SEEM TO STRUGGLE TO SEE IN THEMSELVES, BUT THAT SHINE LIKE A NEON LIGHT TO EVERYONE ELSE IN THEIR WORLD).

Being you – and sharing you with me - is enough."

An Invitation to
Reflect & Respond

When was the last time you apologized for something that didn't require an apology? How often have you offered a "sorry" for things that simply amount to being human—too emotional, too sensitive, too much, or not enough? Take a moment to reflect on the weight of all those apologies and what it's cost you—not just in self-esteem, but in missed opportunities for grace. Who in your life continues to apologize unnecessarily? Can you see in them what they struggle to see in themselves—something wildly beautiful and inherently worthy of compassion? What would it feel like to remove the tally sheets from your life altogether and replace them with unconditional understanding? How might that transform you, your relationships? Your sense of worth and enoughness? Think of someone you care deeply about who routinely apologizes for their existence, their struggles, or their perceived failures. Write them a no-more-"sorry's" letter like the one described. Include your personal version of the "INSERT LIST OF AMAZING TRAITS…" and gift them a permanent permission slip to be human—and loved anyway.

_____

_____

_____

_____

_____

_____

_____

_____

_____

_____

_____

About the Author

Don Blackwell is and, for the past 40 plus years, has been a trial attorney in South Florida. More importantly, Don is the father of two adult children, and "Papa Don" to two amazing grandchildren, Jake and Macie Paige. At various times, Don's also been a little league baseball coach, an afternoon disc jockey, the founder and organizer of a charity golf tournament, an Adjunct Professor of Law, an avid blogger, a noticer, an encourager, a mentor, an outspoken mental health advocate, and the author of numerous articles that have appeared in various local, state, and national publications.

Don's first book, *Dear Ashley: A Father's Reflections and Letters to His Daughter on Life, Love and Hope* (Imbue Press 2013), is a compilation of life lessons learned amid his daughter's decade-long struggle with a life-threatening illness. Since its publication, Don has written and spoken extensively on issues relating to mental health, eating disorders, and compassionate professionalism, making Don a highly sought-after guest on webinars and podcasts tackling those increasingly critical subjects. In 2020, Don organized and hosted the "Legacy of Hope Summit" - a first of its kind symposium attended by more than two dozen highly-respected experts in the eating disorders field aimed at arriving at a blueprint for the path forward in the care and treatment of those illnesses.

Don's second book, *Retune Your Heart – Finding the "Extra" in the Ordinariness of Everyday Life* (2025) is a poignant, often funny, but always insightful collection of nearly 100 stories tracing Don's lifelong quest to dismantle the titanium walls he quite unknowingly constructed around his heart during a highly dysfunctional childhood, and to replace them with the sensitive, inquisitive, and perceptive heart that accompanied him into the world. Don's hope, which he ultimately realized, was that in shedding that armor he would be able to live a more whole and open hearted life marked by a heightened sensitivity to the beauty that all of us encounter, but too often fail to see in the world around us.

That work, in turn, gave birth to *The Playbook of Your Childhood Heart*, a workbook designed to inspire readers to accompany Don on a 13 week journey back to the traits that characterized the hearts that accompanied all of us into the world, before that same world took hold of those hearts and insisted they be more "adult-like."

When he's not spending time with his grandchildren (or working!), Don loves going on long walks, spending time at the beach, engaging in meaningful conversation, playing an occasional round of golf, and listening to classic middle-of-the-road album rock.

Resources

RETUNE YOUR HEART

A beautiful reminder of how the "extra" is everywhere if people are willing to open their eyes and hearts to see it.

GET THE COMPANION WORKBOOK

The Playbook of your Childhood Heart
(a workbook)

Your essential companion for the transformative journey outlined in Donald Blackwell's "Retune Your Heart." Packed with practical exercises, reflections, and actionable steps, it guides you deeper into the core teachings of the book, helping you reconnect with your authentic heart, renew your purpose, and live more intentionally.

for more resources visit retuneyourheart.com

#todolistfridays

Small Weekly Steps to Building a Big-Hearted Life

We're often told that meaningful change requires bold declarations and giant leaps. But what if that story is wrong?

What if lasting change doesn't require you to overhaul your life? What if it can be achieved by taking one small, purposeful step at a time?

> **#todolistfridays** invites and guides you to do just that. To embrace heart-centered growth that's gentle, doable, and real.

Using weekly reflections and simple prompts, #todolistfridays meets you where you are, and makes transformation accessible.

It doesn't require perfection, nor is there a finish line to chase. Just small, intentional steps that, over time, add up to foundational change.

Because the truth sometimes the bravest thing you can do is muster the courage to take the smallest of steps in the right direction.

for more resources visit retuneyourheart.com